What The American Library Association says about *An Ounce of Preservation* . . .

"To collectors of photographs, documents, and books, preservation and conservation — "pres-con" to librarians — present problems pitting the physical needs of perishable materials against the constraints of time and money. Even stopgap measures carry costs, but inept, inadequate, or delayed attention may result in increased deterioration. Here is help for those willing and able to undertake pres-con by themselves. Functioning much as a stylebook does for writers, Tuttle's tidy guide prepares users for undertaking remedial measures. It presents information on paper, inks, environment, storage, and repair simply and clearly; considers the special needs of differing materials; and, in generous appendices and a glossary, helps put users in touch with the specialized world of preservation and conservation. Know-how may not be an absolute substitute for time and money, but a little knowledge can help in taking proactive steps to protect and preserve two-dimensional materials. A valuable resource."

— Mike Tribby
Booklist
The American Library Association

What the Experts Say About An Ounce of Preservation

"Almost every genealogist collects family photographs and documents, and needs to know how to care for them . . . Several books are in print that deal with preservation, but Mr. Tuttle's stands out for its conciseness and readability."

— *The New York Genealogical and Biographical Record*,
The New York Genealogical and Biographical Society

"One of the great fears of the family historian is that a disaster will occur and that something awful will happen to their family research and photographs. Unfortunately, most of the public doesn't see this as a problem and storage of important family documents in the past and even now has been hit and miss at best. Many of our most prized documents and photos from the past find their way to us with significant damage. Now there is help for the layman . . . No genealogist should be without a book on basic preservation techniques and this one covers all the bases in an easily understood fashion . . . to be used by the person who wants and needs to perform basic preservation at home. For such a nominal cost, it should be on the bookshelf of every researcher."

— *Family Records Today*,
American Family Records Association

"Do you know someone who is trying to sift through old boxes of letters and photographs? This helpful book might make the chore easier, and also keep your family mementos from suffering permanent damage . . . really opened my eyes about the way my own papers and photographs should be stored . . . I wish that this book had been available when I first started researching! With good intentions, I laminated certain important family news clippings, which have been totally destroyed in just a few years, due to the destructive processes of lamination. This is a very good book for beginners, but it's never to late for us 'veteran genealogists' to learn, as well . . . Congratulations for a very helpful book!"

— Sandra Lake Lassen,
The Jefferson Post

"This valuable new book is a must have for the collector of anything made of paper . . . "

— Mildred Camp,
The Cookbook Collector

R

An Ounce of Preservation

A Guide to the Care of Papers and Photographs

Craig A. Tuttle

Rainbow Books, Inc.

g-in-Publication Data

to the care of papers and

p. cm.
Includes bibliographical references and index.
ISBN 1-56825-021-5 : $12.95
1. Paper—Preservation. 2. Photographs—Conservation and restoration. I. Title.
TS1109.T88 1994
025.8'4—dc20 94-23044
CIP

An Ounce of Preservation
A Guide to the Care of Papers and Photographs

Published by Rainbow Books, Inc.
P. O. Box 430
Highland City, FL 33846-0430 USA
Editorial Offices Telephone/Fax (941) 648-4420, Email: NAIP@aol.com
Orders: Telephone (800) 356-9315, Fax (800) 242-0036
All photos provided by the author. Photographed materials credited in captions.
Cover and interior design by Betsy A. Lampé

Disclaimer — While the purpose of this book is to assist readers in the care and preservation of their papers and photographs, it is not intended as a substitute for the professional conservation of these materials. If you have any questions or concerns about the condition or treatment of a document or photograph, contact a professional conservator.

Manufactured in the United States of America. Printed on acid-free paper.

ACKNOWLEDGMENTS

I would like to express my appreciation to the following individuals for their invaluable assistance during the writing of this book. First, to Susan Tuttle who read and edited countless drafts of the manuscript and was a constant source of encouragement. To James Schnur, William Thomson and Chong Jue for their helpful comments and suggestions. Lastly, my thanks to Darren Kall, Lisa Purcell, Jeanne Maier and Kenneth Emery for their contribution of documents and photographs that were used in this book.

Contents

INTRODUCTION

As children, my sister and I would often accompany our grandmother to the attic, where she stored the "family treasures." Filled with excitement, we would explore the labyrinth of boxes, dusty furniture and old clothing in search of some forgotten keepsake. Once, we found an old banjo decorated with ink drawings; another time, we discovered a World War I helmet. Later, exhausted from our search, my sister and I would make ourselves comfortable and listen to our grandmother's stories about events and family members long gone.

While cherished as mementos, family papers are also an invaluable source of information for researching medical histories, identifying family relationships and proving ownership of property. In addition, historians frequently use family papers to study the behaviors, thoughts and activities of the people of a particular historical period. The documentary, *The Civil War*, through its extensive use of personal letters, diaries and photographs, illustrated the historical value of family papers. When viewed through the eyes of those who experienced this conflict, the Civil War was no longer a series of battles but a deeply moving, human experience that enables us to better understand and appreciate the enormity of this tragic episode in our history.

This book describes the environmental conditions which cause paper and photograph deterioration, the measures which should be taken to establish a hospitable environment for these materials and recommendations for the proper storage and general care of paper-based items and photographs. In addition, the appendices provide a descriptive list of preservation supplies, where these supplies can be purchased and sources to contact for additional information on paper and photograph preservation. The information in this book will prove useful to anyone interested in preserving paper-based items and photographs. Church secretaries, historical society volunteers, veterans, grandparents, genealogists, historians, librarians, manuscript curators, archivists and collectors will find this book essential.

Lastly, the word "paper," as used in this publication, denotes all types of paper-based items, which include but are not limited to the following: correspondence, books, magazines, comic books, scrapbooks, posters, sports cards, stamps and works of art. In addition, the word "photograph" in this book refers to all photographic materials such as prints, negatives, transparencies and movie film.

Chapter One

What You Need to Know About

PAPER

Historical Overview

The technique of papermaking was invented by Ts'ai Lun in China about 105 A.D. and was introduced to the Middle East in the 8th century by Arab merchants travelling from China via the Silk Route. The technique eventually reached Spain where the first European paper mills were established in the 11th century. During the centuries that followed papermaking spread throughout Europe and, in the late 16th century, to the Americas. The first paper mill in the United States was built in 1690 by William Rittenhouse near Philadelphia, Pennsylvania.

Prior to the introduction of paper, *parchment* (made from sheepskin) and *vellum* (made from calf skin) had been the principal materials used to produce documents and books. However, both parchment and vellum had several drawbacks: they were costly to produce, required lengthy preparation and could only be produced in small quantities due to the limited supply of animal skins. Paper, on the other hand, was inexpensive, easy to manufacture and could be produced in large quantities. Eventually, these factors lead to the advent of paper and a corresponding decline in the use of parchment and vellum.

The increased availability of paper facilitated the growth of literacy and written communication which, in turn, exercised a profound influence on the political, economic and cultural development of society. As societal institutions such as government bureaucracies, business and educational institutions evolved there was an increased use and demand for paper. Papermakers responded to this demand by implementing new methods and technologies to improve paper production. The stamping mill was the first significant innovation to the papermaking process.

Invented in the late 13th century, the *stamping mill* used a series of wooden mallets powered by a water wheel to pound cotton and linen rags into a pulp. Over the centuries, further innovations were made to the papermaking process in response to improvements in printing technology such as the invention of movable type as well as a continued public demand for books and journals. In the late 17th century, the invention of the *Hollander Beater* enabled papermakers to take the first major step toward the mechanization of paper production. This machine accelerated the pulping process by using metal blades to macerate fibers in a manner similar to present day mixers which enabled papermakers to increase their production.

By the end of the 18th century, the number of books, newspapers and other publications had grown so rapidly that papermakers had become increasingly dependent upon technology to meet the continued demand for paper. This situation was resolved in the early 19th century with the invention of the Fourdrinier (1803) and the Cylinder-Mold (1809) papermaking machines. These machines dramatically improved the manufacturing of paper by enabling papermakers to mechanize their operations and, consequently, increase their production of paper.

Although the mechanization of the papermaking process dramatically increased production, by the early 1850s, it had also created a serious shortage of cotton and linen rags, the principal sources of paper fiber. Confronted with these shortages, paper manufacturers began to use wood, which was both abundant and inexpensive, as their principal source of paper fiber. Moreover, to ensure a constant supply of wood, they frequently purchased large tracts of forest. The wood was converted into pulp by a process known as *mechanical pulping*, which consists of grinding wood into short-length fibers, that retains most of the wood-based impurities.

Another method of pulping, invented in the late 1850s, involves the use of chemicals to separate the wood fibers and dissolve the impurities. This process, known as *chemical pulping*, was more costly than mechanical pulping but produced a more durable paper. Further efforts to improve paper production lead manufacturers to increase their use of *alum rosin*, a chemical agent used to size paper (which permits the application of ink). Although introduced to the papermaking process during the late 17th century, alum rosin was not extensively used until the early 19th century. Unlike other sizing agents such as gelatin and starch, which had to be applied to individual sheets of paper, alum rosin was easier to use and more economical because could be added directly to the pulp.

Since the 1850s, paper manufacturers have directed their efforts toward the economical and large-scale production of paper. While these efforts have been successful in producing huge volumes of inexpensive paper, they have also been responsible for the sharp decline in paper quality. However, the decision by paper manufacturers to focus on large scale production was not made arbitrarily but in response to an ever increasing public demand for paper products. Unfortunately, this decline in paper quality has been a principal factor in the rapid deterioration of numerous books, documents and works of art. In the early 1980s, the federal government and the paper industry responded to this problem by forming a committee to establish national standards for paper permanency. The result of the committee's efforts was the creation of the Permanent Paper Standard ANSI Z39 which stated that, to be considered permanent, paper must meet the following requirements:

1. Must have a pH level of 7.5 or greater.
2. Must contain an alkaline buffer of calcium carbonate or another alkaline.
3. Must be free of chemical impurities and, optimally, contain cotton or other rag fibers.
4. Must be resistant to tears and folding.

These standards have lead to the growing production and use of pH-balanced paper for books, magazines, stationary and other paper-based products. The growing use of pH-balanced paper has done much to ensure the longevity of these materials and, ultimately, their use by future generations.

Methods Used in the Production of Paper

The characteristics of paper, i.e. its strength, durability, texture and density, are the direct result of the raw materials and methods used in paper production. In order to appreciate the influence these factors have on paper deterioration it is necessary to understand the processes used to produce paper.

Pulping Processes

Pulping is a process by which fibrous materials are pulverized and mixed with water to form a thick, textured liquid that is used to make paper. Softwoods, such as pine, fir and spruce, are typically used in the production of machine-made paper because their fibers are stronger than hardwoods, and they are easier to pulp. Other fibrous materials, such as cotton and linen, are also used in varying quantities to improve the strength and durability of paper. Conversely, handmade papermaking almost always uses cotton and linen fibers as its primary source of fiber.

Mechanical and *chemical pulping* are the pulping processes used in the manufacture of machine-made paper. Mechanical pulping involves grinding fibrous materials into a pulp while chemical pulping employs various chemicals to facilitate the separation of fibers. The latter process also uses chemical agents to eliminate impurities and improve the texture and color of paper. Alum rosin is used in both mechanical and chemical pulping to permit the application of ink. In addition, paper manufacturers will frequently use variations of these two processes to increase production and improve paper quality.

Mechanical Pulping

Wood is cut lengthwise into sections, soaked in water and tumbled in a drum to remove the bark. The stripped logs are then moved by a conveyor belt to a wet grindstone or grooved metal disks which macerate the wood into short-length fibers. This process can also be adjusted to regulate the length of the fibers. Depending upon the type of paper to be produced, the fibers will then be treated with chemicals to improve their color and texture. In addition, paper manufacturers will sometimes use steam to soften wood fibers prior to their maceration, which causes a small loss in yield but produces a stronger, more durable paper.

Primarily used in the manufacture of inexpensive paper, mechanical pulping produces a short-fibered paper that retains most of its wood-based impurities and residual processing chemicals. Consequently, paper produced from mechanical pulp tends to be weak, less durable and more susceptible to deterioration.

Chemical Pulping

Logs are stripped of their bark, cut up into small chips and then pulverized into fragments by a series of mallets. These wood fragments, along with cotton, linen and other fibrous materials, are placed in vats and then steam heated to facilitate the separation of fibers. Once this has taken place, the pulp is chemically treated with either a sulfite (acid) or sulfate (alkaline) solution to dissolve lignin and other wood-based impurities. Afterward, the pulp is thoroughly washed in water to remove the processing chemicals. Prior to the pulping process, paper manufacturers often treat the wood with chemicals to increase the yield and produce a stronger paper.

Primarily used in the manufacture of high-quality paper, the chemical pulping process produces a paper that is relatively free of chemicals and wood-based impurities. Paper produced by this method is strong, durable and has a greater resistance to deterioration.

Handmade Paper

Handmade paper involves the manual pounding of fibrous material such as cotton and linen rags until the fibers have separated into long strands. Placed in large vats of water, the fibers bond together to form a watery pulp called slurry. Paper molds, fitted with tightly woven screens, are then dipped into the slurry and manipulated until an even layer of pulp lies on the screen. After the excess water has been allowed to drain, the layer of pulp is removed and placed between pieces of absorbent fabric. When dry, the layer of pulp forms a sheet of paper that is sized (coated) with either gelatin, glue or starch to permit the application of ink.

Machine-made Paper

The processes used to manufacture machine-made paper are fundamentally the same as those used to produce handmade paper. However, the production of machine-made paper consists of manufacturing operations that are extensive, extremely sophisticated and directed toward large-scale paper production. Conversely, handmade papermaking is a comparatively limited operation that produces smaller quantities of paper. The types of machinery used in the manufacture of paper are the *Fourdrinier* and the *Cylinder-Mold machines*, which are described below.

Fourdrinier Machine

This machine mechanically pours the pulp onto a finely meshed, horizontal metal screen that drains the water and vibrates from side to side to permit an even layer of pulp. The pulp is then carried to cylinders which remove the excess water and smooth the pulp to form a continuous roll of paper. Depending on the type of paper being produced, a dandy roll will be used to give each sheet a watermark. The paper is then transported through a number of steam-heated driers and, finally, to a calendar roll, which gives the paper a smooth finish. When the process is completed, the paper is rolled, stored and later cut to size.

The Fourdrinier machine is primarily used to produce commercial letterhead and stationary, inexpensive book paper and newsprint from either mechanical pulp or a mixture of mechanical and chemical pulp. Equipped to manufacture paper in high volume, the Fourdrinier machine produces poor- to good-quality paper.

Cylinder-Mold Machine

This machine pours the pulp into a vat that contains a partially immersed, cylindrical drum equipped with a finely meshed metal screen. As the drum revolves, the pulp is deposited on the screen and then transported to a series of felt-covered, metal cylinders which squeeze out the excess water. The paper is then transported through a series of steam-heated driers and, finally, to a calender roll, which gives the paper a smooth surface. When the process is completed, the paper is rolled, stored and later cut to size.

The Cylinder-Mold machine is primarily used to produce high-quality letterhead, stationary, ledger paper, securities and currency from chemically pulped wood, cotton and linen rags. Although the Cylinder-Mold machine has a higher cost of production and a lower output than the Fourdrinier process, it produces paper that is both strong and durable.

Chapter Two

What You Need to Know About

INKS

Historical Overview

Ink was first used in ancient Egypt about 2500 B.C. and consisted of *lampblack* (carbon) mixed in a solution of water and natural gums. This type of ink continued to be used for centuries with little modification. However, in the 15th century, the growing desire for books and other publications encouraged printers to add varnish and linseed oil, which enabled the ink to dry more quickly and, thus, allowed printers to increase their production. By the mid 19th century, printers and ink makers had introduced a variety of chemical agents, pigments and solvents to improve the color, texture and flow of ink. Mineral oils were also used during this period to facilitate the printing of books and newspapers. During the 20th century, various synthetic pigments, resins and solvents were introduced to the manufacture of writing and printing inks.

Documents, whatever their format, have one common element: they are written or printed with ink. Ink is not only essential to communicate information but is an influential factor in the preservation of paper. While some types of ink are durable, others stimulate chemical reactions which cause paper to deteriorate. The section below discusses the composition of inks and their resistance to adverse environmental conditions.

Writing Inks

Prior to the 20th century, most writing inks were either *carbon-* or *oak-gall-based solutions*. Carbon-based inks are composed of carbon, natural gums and water. Still used by artists and calligraphers, carbon-based ink is extremely durable and resistant to the deteriorative effects of humidity, air and light. Iron Gall ink, used from the 17th to the early 20th century, is a mixture of iron sulfate, oak galls, arabic gum and water. Unlike carbon-based inks, iron gall is acidic, fades to varying shades of brown and eventually burns through paper.

Present-day inks used in ball-point, fountain and felt-tip pens are composed of synthetic solvents, resins and dyes which have a low to moderate resistance to excessive humidity and light. These inks, when exposed to adverse environmental conditions for prolonged periods of time, will fade, run and stimulate chemical reactions which accelerate paper deterioration.

Printing Inks

Prior to the mid 19th century, printing inks were composed of carbon, natural pigments, varnish and linseed oil. These inks are highly resistant to light, air and humidity and retain much of their original appearance. Modern printing inks, on the other hand, contain a variety of synthetic dyes, resins and solvents. The specific properties of these inks vary based on their intended use and the perceived value of the item. For example, newspapers are printed with fast-drying, inexpensive inks while engraved invitations are produced with more costly, slow-drying and thick-textured inks. In general, modern printing inks are long lasting but will deteriorate when exposed to adverse environmental conditions for prolonged periods of time.

Typewriter, Laser Printer and Copy Machine Inks

These inks are composed of various synthetic dyes, resins and solvents, which have a moderate resistance to the deteriorative effects of light, humidity and air.

Chapter Three

What You Need to Know About

PHOTOGRAPHS

Historical Overview

The introduction of the *daguerreotype* photograph in 1839 not only established a distinctive medium to record people, places and events, but one that could also convey and elicit a variety of emotions and ideas. From the beginning, there was an enormous public demand for photographs, and people flocked to photograph studios to have their likenesses preserved in portrait. Almost overnight, photograph studios began to appear in major cities and small towns, while travelling photographers plied their trade in the rural areas.

While photography gained widespread popularity for producing portraits, it was also used to record other subject matter, such as landscapes, cities, works of art and foreign lands. Photographs depicting these subjects were extremely popular with the public, who found them both entertaining and educational. The invention of the *stereograph* photograph (which gave the illusion of a three-dimensional image when viewed through a stereoscope) further increased the public demand for these types of photographs.

The commercial success of photography also encouraged many of its practitioners to simplify the picture-taking process and improve the image quality of photographs. Consequently, numerous technological innovations were made to both photographic processes and equipment which enhanced the versatility and the image quality of photographs. These improvements not only enabled photographers to devote more attention to their subjects but also encouraged larger numbers of people to take an active interest in photography.

By the 1850s, these innovations had also helped to establish a new form of photography: *photojournalism*. Initially, the use of this type of photography was hampered by the technical limitations of newspapers, which could only reproduce photographs in the form of wood engravings. The outbreak of the Civil War in 1861 had an enormous impact on the growth of photojournalism and the use of photography for military surveillance. Many photographers realized the value of photography for documenting the war and quickly applied to the federal government for permission to travel with the army. The most notable of these photographers were Matthew Brady, Alexander Gardner and Timothy O'Sullivan, who left their lucrative portrait studios to photograph the conflict. The photographs produced during the Civil War were harsh, often brutal, in their depiction of the death and destruction, and they frequently expressed the photographer's personal sentiments about the events they had witnessed. The public response to these photographs was one of horror and disgust, and it forever shattered their romanticized image of war.

In the years following the Civil War, photojournalism underwent an expansive growth that was greatly facilitated, in the 1880s, by the invention of the *halftone process*. This process, which used various-sized black dots, enabled photographs to be reproduced in newspapers, books and magazines. During this period, there was also a growing use of photography as a means of social commentary. Jacob Riis, a crusading newspaper reporter during the 1880s, was a pioneer of this type of photography. The photographs taken by Riis were extremely effective in publicizing the horrific living and working conditions of the urban poor and were influential in introducing legislation that eventually reformed these conditions.

By the late 1880s, the nature of photography had undergone a dramatic change with the introduction of a small, plain-looking box camera called the *Kodak No. 1*. Unlike its predecessors, this camera was light weight, easy to operate, and came pre-loaded with film. After exposure, the film and camera were sent to the manufacturer, which developed the film, made prints and reloaded the camera. Extremely popular with the public, the Kodak No. 1 shifted the use of photography from a relatively small body of professional and talented amateurs to anyone capable of holding a camera and pressing a button. The Kodak No. 1 camera also encouraged further innovations to cameras, and other photographic equipment, to facilitate their use by the public. Although photographic processes continued to be refined, there were no major innovations until 1935 when Kodak introduced the first practical color transparency, *Kodachrome*. A great commercial success, Kodachrome was followed by the introduction of color movie film, in 1938, and color film and prints in 1942.

Another major innovation to the photographic process was *Polaroid film*. Introduced in 1947 by Edwin Land, Polaroid film enabled a black and white image to be developed within seconds after exposure by using a specially equipped camera. The Polaroid Company continued to improve on the process and, by 1963, had introduced a color film. Over the years, technological improvements have continued to refine photographic processes and equipment, which has made it possible to view photographic images on computer screens, television sets and enabled us to view distant planets.

Composition of Photographs

Structurally, a photograph consists of an *emulsion* (light-sensitive layer), a *base* (composed of plastic film, paper or another material which supports the emulsion) and an *adhesive* that secures the emulsion to the base. An emulsion contains particles of light-sensitive silver salts suspended in a layer of gelatin. When exposed to light, the silver salts in the emulsion are transformed into minute grains of black, metallic silver, which form an image. Chemical solutions are then used to develop and stabilize ("fix") the image. Afterward, the photograph is washed in water to remove any residual chemicals.

Unfortunately, the standard processing methods used by many photo labs leave a residue of silver salts and chemicals on photographs, negatives, transparencies and movie film which have a deteriorative effect on photographic emulsions. Unexposed silver salts absorb light, which causes the image to darken, while residual chemicals leave discolorations. In addition, these chemicals interact with environmental factors such as light, pollution and humidity, all of which accelerate the deterioration of photographic materials. The damage caused by residual salts and chemicals can be prevented by the *archival processing* of negatives and photographs. This process, offered by many photo labs, thoroughly removes residual silver salts and chemicals from photographic materials and uses various chemical compounds to shield the image from external contaminants. While archival processing is more expensive than its commercial counterpart, it provides a greater degree of protection from deterioration.

Major Photographic Processes

The section below provides a comprehensive description of the major photographic processes used since the invention of photography and will be helpful in the identification of photographs.

Calotype

Calotype, also known as *Talbotype* (period of use: 1835-mid 1850s), was invented by William Talbot several years before the introduction of the daguerreotype. The calotype process involved the application of silver iodide (a light-sensitive solution) to a sheet of paper that was placed in a camera, exposed and then developed in a solution of gallic acid to produce a negative image. Afterward, another sheet of sensitized paper was used to make a positive print from the negative. Unfortunately, the calotype process produced photographs with grainy images which were unable to compete with the sharp image quality of the daguerreotype. Consequently, the calotype process was never wholly accepted by the public. By the mid 1850s, the calotype process was replaced by the collodion process. Calotypes can be identified by the dull, grainy quality of their images.

Daguerreotype

Daguerreotype (period of use: 1839-mid 1850s), named after its inventor, Louis Daguerre, was the first commercially successful photographic process. The daguerreotype process produced a direct positive image by using a copper plate that was coated with silver, polished and then exposed to iodine vapors to make it light sensitive. The plate was placed in a camera, exposed and then heated over a pan of mercury to produce a sharp, detailed image. Fragile and easily damaged, daguerreotypes were usually inserted in wooden cases to protect the images. While daguerreotypes were extremely popular, the process could not duplicate images, which eventually lead to its decline. By the mid 1850s, the daguerreotype had been replaced by the collodion process. Daguerreotypes can be identified by their mirror-like quality, which requires the viewer to hold them at certain angles of light to see the image as a positive.

Albumen Process

Albumen Process (period of use: 1847-mid 1890s) involved the preparation of egg whites, sodium chloride and silver nitrate. Coated on glass plate negatives, this process yielded finely detailed images but required exceedingly long exposures (from five to fifteen minutes). Although frequently used for photographing landscapes and buildings, the long exposures of the albumen process precluded its use in portrait photography. However, the introduction of albumen-sensitized paper in 1850 enabled this process to be used to produce sharp, high-resolution portrait photographs from collodion negatives. Albumen prints were commonly referred to as *card photographs* because they were usually mounted on various-sized cards to prevent the thin paper print from curling or tearing. This format was extremely popular from the mid 1850s to the 1910s and was used to produce the following types of card photographs:

Albumen prints were mounted on cardboard to prevent the print from curling or tearing. (courtesy of the author)

- ❖ *Cartes-de-viste* — which measures 2¼ by 4¼ inches and was popular from the mid 1850s to late 1860s.
- ❖ *Cabinet card* — which measures 4¼ by 6½ inches and was popular from the mid 1860s to 1900.
- ❖ *Victoria card* — which measures 3¼ by 5

inches and was popular from the early 1870s to late 1880s.

- *Promenade card* — which measures 4 by 7 inches and was popular from the mid 1870s to the late 1890s.
- *Imperial card* — which measures 7 7/8 by 9 7/8 inches and was popular from the late 1870s to 1900.
- *Boudoir card* — which measures 5 by 8 ¼ inches and was popular from the late 1870s to 1900.
- *Stereograph card* — which measures 3 x 7 inches and was popular from the late 1850s to late 1910s. Two identical images were mounted on this card to create a three-dimensional effect when viewed through a stereoscope.

While albumen print paper continued to be used until the mid 1890s, most card photographs by the late 1880s were produced on paper that contained a dry gelatin emulsion. Albumen photographs can be identified by the yellowish highlights in their images.

Collodion Process

Collodion Process (period of use: 1851-1890s) involved the preparation of guncotton fibers, potassium iodide, silver nitrate, alcohol and ether. Commonly referred to as the "*wet plate*" process, the exposure and development of collodion negatives had to be completed while the emulsion was still wet, usually fifteen minutes. The collodion process was highly regarded for the sharp detail and rich contrast of its images and was used to produce the following:

Ambrotypes were produced by applying the collodion solution to polished glass. (courtesy of the author)

- *Ambrotypes* (period of use: 1854-1870s) — which were made by coating the collodion solution on polished glass that, when exposed, produced a negative. The image was made to appear as a positive by placing black-colored paper, fabric or metal behind the glass negative, which was framed, and then placed in a wooden case. Ambrotypes were produced in a variety of sizes ranging from 2 1/2 x 3 1/2 to 8 x 10 inches. Extremely popular from the 1850s to mid 1860s, ambrotypes were easier to produce and less expensive than daguerreotypes. Although similar in appearance to daguerreotypes, ambrotypes do not have the latter's mirror-like surface.

Tintypes were produced by applying the collodion solution to lacquered metal. (courtesy of the author)

❖ *Tintypes* (period of use: 1856- late 1890s) — which were made by coating the collodion solution on a thin sheet of lacquered metal to produce a direct, positive image. Primarily used in portrait photography, tintypes were highly regarded for their durability, low cost and quick development. Their image quality, however, lacked the crisp resolution of the ambrotype. Tintypes were produced in sizes which ranged from 1/2 x 1/2 to 3 1/2 x 4 1/2 inches. These photographs were placed in albums, jewelry and, occasionally, wooden cases. Although the popularity of the tintype declined in the mid 1870s, they continued to be produced until the late 1890s. Tintypes can be identified by their dull, grayish images and metal base, which is either black or chocolate-brown in color.

- *Wet Plate Negatives* (period of use: 1851-early 1890s) — which were made on various sizes of hand-cut, glass plates coated with the collodion solution. These negatives were primarily used to make photographic prints on albumen-sensitized paper. The collodion "wet plate" process was the standard method used to produce negatives until early 1880s when it was replaced by the dry gelatin emulsion process. Collodion negatives can be identified by the greyish color and uneven texture of their emulsions.

Dry Gelatin Process

Dry Gelatin Process (period of use: 1871-present) involved the use of nitro cellulose, chloride and silver halides suspended in a layer of gelatin. Unlike previous processes, gelatin emulsions did not require any preparation by the photographer, and they were more sensitive to light, which enabled exposure times to be reduced to fractions of a second. Gelatin emulsions were first used on glass plate negatives but, by 1889, were being manufactured on paper and celluloid film. Glass plate gelatin emulsions can be identified by the blackish highlights in their images and the smooth texture of the emulsion. The dry gelatin emulsion process has been used to produce the following:

The dry gelatin process provided the first "ready-to-use" emulsion. Dry gelatin emulsions were initially produced on glass plate negatives. (courtesy of the author)

Cellulose Nitrate Film (period of use: 1888-1951) — which was the first generation of gelatin emulsion to be manufactured on celluloid film. Unfortunately, cellulose nitrate has proven to be a chemically unstable and highly flammable film that will spontaneously deteriorate at a rapid rate. For these reasons, it is highly recommended that cellulose nitrate film be copied and then disposed of properly. Since local fire ordinances regard this type of film as a hazardous waste, it is recommended that your local fire department be contacted for information on its proper disposal. Cellulose nitrate film can be identified by the word "nitrate" located at the film's edge and its acrid odor.

Cellulose Acetate Film (period of use: 1937-mid 1960s) — was the first generation of "safety film" and replaced the highly flammable substance "nitrate" with "diacetate." Unfortunately, cellulose diacetate will also self-destruct due to chemical reactions which form wrinkles and small bubbles in the emulsion. Film displaying this type of damage should be copied immediately. Cellulose triacetate film and polyester film, introduced in the late 1940s and early 1960s, respectively, do not have this problem and are extremely stable. Cellulose acetate film can be identified by the word "safety" located on the edge of the film.

Color Film and Photographs (period of use: 1935-present) — were developed as early as the late 1890s, but numerous technical flaws made these materials unreliable and extremely difficult to use. In 1935, Eastman Kodak introduced Kodachrome, the first practical and easy-to-use color process. A transparency film, Kodachrome consisted of several layers of color dyes and other chemicals suspended in a gelatin base. The commercial success of Kodachrome was followed, in 1938, with the introduction of color movie film and, in 1942, with a color negative and print process. Over the years, numerous improvements have been made to color film and photographs which have enhanced their image quality and stability. However, despite these improvements, the chemicals used in color film and photographs still undergo chemical changes which, over time, alter the color of their images. In addition, environmental factors such as light, pollution and humidity will accelerate this deteriorative process.

Polaroid Film

Polaroid Film (period of use: 1947-present) is an innovative process that involves the use of chemicals contained in pods to form an image. After exposure, these chemicals are released by passing the film through rollers in the camera which enables the photograph to be developed and stabilized ("fixed") within seconds. Initially, the process could only produce black and white photographs. However, by 1963, the Polaroid Company had introduced a color version of the process. Polaroid film has one drawback in that it can only be used in Polaroid cameras.

Chapter Four

How to Recognize and Treat DETERIORATION

Introduction

The deterioration of paper and photographs is influenced by the interdependent relationship that exists between the environment and the chemical stability of these items. Within this relationship, the environment plays a more important role because it functions as a catalyst to either initiate or inhibit deterioration and, moreover, can be controlled. The chemical stability of papers and photographs, determined by the materials and processes used in their production, represents the capacity of these materials to resist deterioration caused by the environment.

Adverse environmental conditions expose papers and photographs to a variety of chemical compounds that alter or undermine their chemical composition which results in the deterioration of these items. The harshness of the environment conditions, length of exposure and chemical stability of the items also determine the speed and severity of this deterioration. A hospitable environment, on the other hand, is beneficial to the preservation of papers and photographs because it creates conditions that prevent or, at a minimum, discourage the formation of destructive chemical compounds. This type of environment not only protects papers and photographs from deterioration but also greatly enhances their longevity.

The principal chemical reactions caused by the environment are *oxidation* and the *formation of acidic chemical compounds*. Both of these processes undermine the chemical stability of paper and photographs and, consequently, cause them to deteriorate. Oxidation occurs when oxygen bonds with the chemicals in paper and photographs

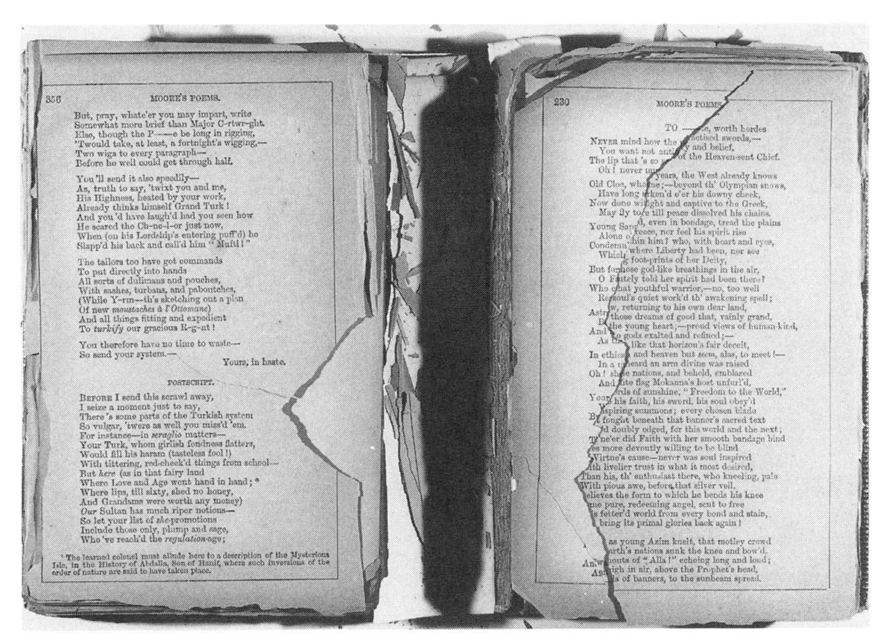

356 MOORE'S POEMS.

But, pray, whate'er you may impart, write
Somewhat more brief than Major C-rtwr-ght.
Else, though the P——e be long in rigging,
'Twould take, at least, a fortnight's wigging,—
Two wigs to every paragraph—
Before he well could get through half.

You 'll send it also speedily—
As, truth to say, 'twixt you and me,
His Highness, heated by your work,
Already thinks himself Grand Turk!
And you 'd have laugh'd had you seen how
He scared the Ch-nc-l-or just now,
When (on his Lordship's entering puff'd) he
Slapp'd his back and call'd him "Mufti!"

The tailors too have got commands
To put directly into hands
All sorts of dulimans and pouches,
With sashes, turbans, and paboutches,
(While Y-rm—th's sketching out a plan
Of new *moustaches à l'Ottomane*)
And all things fitting and expedient
To *turkify* our gracious R-g-nt!

You therefore have no time to waste—
So send your system.—
Yours, in haste.

POSTSCRIPT.

BEFORE I send this scrawl away,
I seize a moment just to say,
There 's some parts of the Turkish system
So vulgar, 'twere as well you miss'd 'em.
For instance—in *seraglio* matters—
Your Turk, whom girlish fondness flatters,
Would fill his haram (tasteless fool!)
With tittering, red-cheek'd things from school—
But *here* (as in that fairy land
Where Love and Age went hand in hand;*
Where lips, till sixty, shed no honey,
And Grandams were worth any money)
Our Sultan has much riper notions—
So let your list of *she*-promotions
Include those only, plump and sage,
Who 've reach'd the *regulation*-age;

* The learned colonel must allude here to a description of the Mysterious Isle, in the History of Abdalla, Son of Hanif, where such inversions of the order of nature are said to have taken place.

230 MOORE'S POEMS.

TO ——e, worth hordes
NEVER mind how the [illegible]ctised swords,—
You want not anti[illegible]y and belief,
The lip that 's so [illegible] of the Heaven-sent Chief.
Oh! never [illegible] years, the West already knows
Old Cloe, who[illegible]ne;—beyond th' Olympian snows,
Have long [illegible]ken'd o'er his downy cheek,
Now done wi[illegible]ght and captive to the Greek,
May fly to[illegible]e till peace dissolved his chains,
Young Sap[illegible]d, even in bondage, tread the plains
Alone o[illegible]reece, nor feel his spirit rise
Condemn[illegible]hin him? who, with heart and eyes,
Which[illegible] where Liberty had been, nor see
[illegible]g foot-prints of her Deity,
But fo[illegible]hose god-like breathings in the air,
O F[illegible]ntely told her spirit had been there?
Who [illegible]hat youthful warrior,—no, too well
Re[illegible]soul's quiet work'd th' awakening spell;
[illegible]w, returning to his own dear land,
Astr[illegible] those dreams of good that, vainly grand,
D[illegible] the young heart,—proud views of human-kind,
And [illegible] to gods exalted and refined;—
As [illegible] like that horizon's fair deceit,
In ethic[illegible] and heaven but *seem*, alas, to meet!—
In a [illegible]heard an arm divine was raised
Oh! sh[illegible]e nations, and beheld, emblazed
And [illegible]ite flag Mokanna's host unfurl'd,
[illegible]rds of sunshine, "Freedom to the World,"
Your[illegible] his faith, his sword, his soul obey'd
[illegible]spiring summons; every chosen blade
By[illegible] fought beneath that banner's sacred text
[illegible]d doubly edged, for this world and the next;
T[illegible] ne'er did Faith with her smooth bandage bind
[illegible]es more devoutly willing to be blind
[illegible]Virtue's cause—never was soul inspired
[illegible]ith livelier trust in what it most desired,
Than his, th' enthusiast there, who kneeling, pale
With pious awe, before that silver veil,
[illegible]elieves the form to which he bends his knee
[illegible]me pure, redeeming angel, sent to free
[illegible]s fetter'd world from every bond and stain,
[illegible] bring its primal glories back again!

[illegible] as young Azim knelt, that motley crowd
[illegible]arth's nations sunk the knee and bow'd,
An[illegible] w[illegible]outs of "Alla!" echoing long and loud;
A[illegible]igh in air, above the Prophet's head,
[illegible]s of banners, to the sunbeam spread.

Oxidation has slowly "burned" the pages in this book to a chocolate brown color. (courtesy of the author)

to form new chemical compounds which cause these materials to deteriorate. The rate of oxidation can vary depending on the environmental conditions. A sheet of white paper that has caught fire is an example of extremely rapid oxidation. As the paper burns, its color changes from white, to light brown, to black as the carbohydrates in the cellulose fiber are transformed into carbon dioxide. Consequently, the physical structure of the paper is transformed to an ash-like substance. Slower rates of oxidation cause paper and photographs to become yellow to dark brown in color and brittle to the touch. While oxidation is a natural and inevitable process, it can be slowed down by maintaining an environment that is beneficial to the preservation of paper and photographs.

The formation of acids is another serious threat to paper and photographs that occurs when the residual chemicals in these materials bond with other chemicals to produce highly acidic compounds, which cause paper and photographs to become weak, brittle and discolored. The acidity in one document or photograph can also be transferred to another item through physical contact or exposure to acidic vapors in a process commonly referred to as *acid migration*. In addition, acids by weakening the chemical bonds in paper and photographs, facilitates their deterioration by oxidation.

The section below discusses the environmental conditions which accelerate the deterioration of paper and photographs, the specific types of damage caused by these conditions and the measures which can be implemented for their prevention and treatment.

Temperature and Relative Humidity

Temperature is a standard measurement used to determine the degree of hotness or coldness in an environment while *relative humidity* indicates the percentage of moisture in the air relative to the maximum amount the air can hold at that temperature. An excessively high or low temperature and relative humidity will stimulate chemical reactions which cause paper and photographs to deteriorate.

Under conditions of high temperature and relative humidity, the cellulose fibers in paper and photographs absorb excess moisture in the air, stimulating water-based chemical reactions which produce acids, accelerate oxidation and encourage fungal growth. Paper and photographs exposed to these conditions become weak, moldy and waterstained. In addition, photographic emulsions will soften and separate from their support. Conversely, low levels of temperature and relative humidity stimulate cellulose fibers to release water vapor, which causes the fibers to physi-

Excessively high levels of humidity have severely damaged this tintype, which has caused a substantial loss of its image. (courtesy of Darren Kall and Lisa Purcell)

The water stains and mold growth on this print are the result of prolonged exposure to excessively humid conditions. (courtesy of the author)

cally deteriorate. Paper and photographs exposed to such conditions become dry, brittle and dark in color. In addition, photographs will curl because their emulsions tend to contract more than their paper support. Extreme fluctuations in temperature and humidity are also detrimental because they cause cellulose fibers and photographic emulsions to swell and contract in response to changing climate conditions. These fluctuations create enormous physical stress that will cause paper and photographs to wrinkle and accelerate their deterioration.

Moderate levels of temperature and relative humidity create conditions that are stable and, therefore, beneficial to the preservation of papers and photographs. Optimally, the temperature and relative humidity in your storage area should be between 65-68 degrees Fahrenheit and 45-50 percent. An acceptable, but less desirable, range of temperature and relative humidity is 69-72 degrees Fahrenheit and 51-55 percent. *Silica gel canisters* are recommended to absorb moisture caused by excessive humidity.

Signs of Damage

- ❖ Documents and photographs which are weak, brittle and discolored.
- ❖ Documents which have water stains or inks that have run.
- ❖ Documents and photographs which are curled, wrinkled or stuck together.
- ❖ Photographic emulsions which have wrinkled or separated from their base.

Preventative Measures and Treatment

Set the thermostat in your home or, if possible, the storage area to one of the recommended ranges below:

❖ *Optimal:* 65-68 degrees Fahrenheit
45-50% Relative Humidity

❖ *Acceptable:* 69-71 degrees Fahrenheit
51-55% Relative Humidity

Photographs which exhibit a minimal degree of curling and are in good condition can be flattened by following a technique described in the chapter, "How to Perform Simple Repair and Cleaning."

Photographs, negatives, transparencies and movie film which have been stored in temperatures below 32 degrees Fahrenheit should be gradually exposed to warmer temperatures to prevent condensation from forming on their surfaces.

Fungi, Insects and Rodents

Mold and other types of *fungi* are another cause of paper and photograph deterioration. Always present in the air, fungi are most active when the air is stagnant, the temperature exceeds 75 degrees Fahrenheit and the relative humidity is above 60 percent. Stagnant air enables fungal spores to settle on papers and photographs while excessive climatic conditions encourage the spores to germinate. Once this occurs, fungi continue to grow by digesting the carbohydrates and other organic substances in paper, photographs and the leather bindings of books. Fungi will also interact with the iron salts in paper. This particular type of fungal damage is known as *foxing* and leaves reddish-brown spots on paper. In addition, many types of fungi excrete acids which further damage paper and photographs. Fungal damage causes paper to become weak, limp and to easily break apart when handled, and it will obscure photographic images beyond recognition.

Insects and *rodents* will also cause serious damage to paper and photographs. These vermin, which prefer a warm, humid climate, digest the organic substances contained in paper, photographs and the leather bindings of books. Insects and rodents can literally eat through stacks of paper while rodents, in particular, will shred paper and photographs for use as nesting material. Paper and photographs exposed to insect and rodent infestation exhibit small to crater-like holes and dark, encrusted spots (droppings) which are acidic.

Mold growth, caused by excessive humidity and stagnant air, has severely damaged this photograph. (courtesy of Darren Kall and Lisa Purcell)

This page of sheet music has been severely stained by mold growth. (courtesy of Jeanne Maier)

The types of insects and rodents which commonly cause paper and photographs to deteriorate are listed below:

Insects and rodents have caused substantial damage to the leather cover of this book. (courtesy of the author)

- *Insects* — Cockroaches, silverfish, bookworms, lice and mites, termites and moths.
- *Rodents* — Mice, rats and squirrels.

Prevention is the best way to protect paper and photographs from fungal, insect and rodent damage. The temperature and relative humidity in your storage area should be set to one of the two ranges described in "Temperature and Relative Humidity." Furthermore, use a fan or an air conditioner to maintain a constant circulation of air. Avoid leaving food or beverages in your storage area which will attract insects and rodents. In addition, periodically inspect your materials for signs of infestation and, if present, contact an exterminator or spray the area with insecticides. However, *be sure that the insecticides do not come into direct contact with your materials*. Early stages of fungal growth on documents can be removed with a soft cotton cloth while early fungal growth on photographs, negatives, transparencies and movie film can usually be removed with a non-water-based film cleaner. However, this *film cleaner should not be used on daguerreotypes, ambrotypes, tintypes or glass plate negatives*. Paper and photographs which exhibit more advanced stages of fungal growth should be treated by a conservator.

Signs of Damage

- Documents and photographs with brown or reddish-brown fibrous spots.
- Documents which are limp and easily break apart when

handled.

- Photographic images which are obscured.
- Documents and photographs with dark, encrusted spots, small to crater-like holes or which have been shredded.

Preventative Measures and Treatment

- Maintain the climate ranges recommended in "Temperature and Relative Humidity."
- Do not leave food or beverages in your storage area.
- Use a fan or an air conditioner to maintain a constant circulation of air.
- Brush off early stages of fungal growth on paper with a soft cotton cloth.
- Use a non-water-based cleaner to remove early stages of fungal growth on photographs, negatives, transparencies and movie film. *Film cleaner should not be used on daguerrèotypes, ambrotypes, tintypes or glass plate negatives.*
- Periodically inspect materials for insect or rodent infestation and, if present, contact an exterminator. *Be sure that the insecticides do not come into direct contact with your materials.*

Light Exposure

Light contains energized particles called photons which stimulate chemical reactions in paper and photographs which result in the deterioration of these materials. While all forms of illumination are harmful, most of the damage to paper and photographs is caused by *ultraviolet radiation* and *light-generated heat.* Ultraviolet radiation undermines the chemical bonds in paper and photographs, which increases their susceptibility to oxidation and acids. Light-generated heat, on the other hand, dehydrates the cellulose fibers in paper and photographs, which causes these materials to lose their lubricant-like resiliency and tensile strength. Sunlight and, to a lesser degree, fluorescent light are the most destructive forms of illumination because they contain the highest levels of ultraviolet radiation, and they generate the most intense levels of heat. Incandescent light also gener-

Prolonged exposure to light has caused the images in this stereograph photograph to darken almost beyond recognition. (courtesy of Darren Kall and Lisa Purcell)

ates intense heat but emits negligible amounts of ultraviolet radiation.

Light damage is cumulative and is influenced by the length and intensity of exposure. Interestingly, paper and photographs which are exposed to short periods of intense light undergo a similar degree of deterioration as those exposed to prolonged periods of low-level light exposure. The deteriorative effects of light will bleach or darken paper and cause it to become embrittled. Light also causes inks to fade, darkens black and white photographs and chemically alters the dyes in color photographs, negatives and movie film.

The following measures can help minimize the damaging effects of sun and fluorescent light:

- ❖ Use venetian blinds and curtains to restrict the exposure of sun light to your storage area.
- ❖ Use ultraviolet filters on windows and fluorescent lights to eliminate the deteriorative effects of ultraviolet radiation.
- ❖ Use low-watt incandescent bulbs, for example, 60 watts. This type of light emits far less ultraviolet radiation than fluorescent light, but it should be placed at a distance of at least four feet from your materials.
- ❖ Place paper and photographs in pH-balanced storage boxes.
- ❖ Limit the amount of light exposure to your materials.

Signs of Damage

- ❖ Documents which are weak, brittle and yellow to dark brown in color.
- ❖ Ink that has faded.
- ❖ Photographs which have a metallic sheen, are darkened, faded, cracked or have undergone changes in color.

Preventative Measures and Treatment

- ❖ Minimize the duration and intensity of sun and fluorescent light to your materials.
- ❖ Use venetian blinds and curtains to restrict the exposure of sun light to your storage area.
- ❖ Place papers and photographs in pH-balanced storage boxes.
- ❖ Use ultraviolet filters on windows and fluorescent lights.
- ❖ Use low watt incandescent light bulbs, e.g. 60 watts, and place them at a distance of at least four feet from your materials.

Surface dirt and pollutants have severely marred this photograph. (courtesy of Darren Kall and Lisa Purcell)

Pollutants

Pollutants stimulate chemical reactions in paper and photographs which produce destructive acids and accelerate oxidation. Atmospheric pollutants, created by industrial and automobile emissions, contain destructive gases and solid particles, such as dirt, dust and soot. Gaseous atmospheric pollutants bond with oxygen to produce corrosive chemical compounds which leave paper and photographs weak, brittle and stained. Solid particles are also destructive because they abrade paper surfaces and photographic emulsions. Pollutants also emanate from various household products, solvents and paints whose fumes have a deteriorative effect on paper and photographs; even burning wood and tobacco are detrimental. In addition, pollutants will cause permanent smudge marks and fingerprints on documents and photographs when they mix with the oils excreted from our fingers.

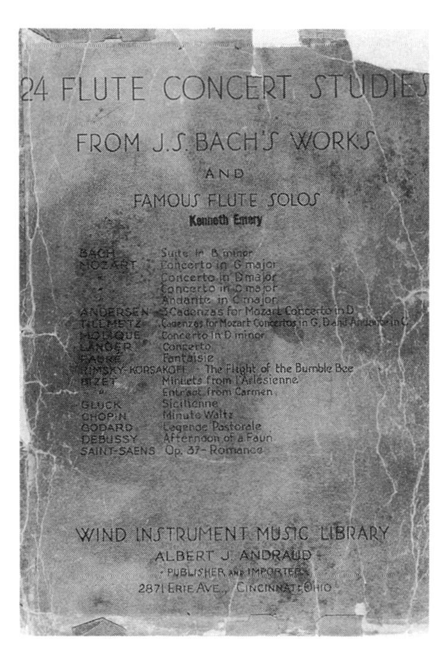

The cover of this book of sheet music has been severely damaged by pollutants. (courtesy of Kenneth Emery)

Most pollutants can be eliminated with an air purifier. These units generate negative ions that attach themselves to the positively charged pollutants and entrap them in charcoal filters. Air purifiers are available in a number of makes and models which have varying degrees of effectiveness. The cost of these units range from about $100 to $500. Air conditioner units are also useful for cleansing the air of pollutants but have several drawbacks: they are very costly to operate, their use is limited to the warmer months of the year, and they are not as effective. When selecting an air purifier, the following factors should be considered:

- *Range* — The size of the area (in square feet) that a unit can effectively cleanse. Select a unit that meets or exceeds the size requirements for your storage area.
- *Frequency of Purification* — The number of times the area is cleansed within a one-hour period. At a minimum, the unit should cleanse the area three times an hour.
- *Charcoal Filters* — These filters are used to entrap airborne pollutants. For effective cleansing, an air purifier should have at least two charcoal filters. Do not purchase air purifiers which lack a filtering system. These units

will leave a soot-like buildup on the walls, the furniture and the carpet near the unit.

- ❖ *Ozone Emissions* — Select an air purifier that does not emit ozone.
- ❖ *Maintenance Cost* — The expense of filter replacement and electricity varies between air purifiers. At a maximum, filters should only require replacement every three months. The cost of operating an air purifier varies, so it is important to check the unit for its annual cost of operation.

The presence of solid particles can also be reduced by vacuuming your storage area on a biweekly basis. Papers and photographs which are covered with a layer of dust, dirt or soot should be cleaned with a soft-haired brush to prevent scratching their surfaces. It is also important to wash your hands, or use latex or cotton gloves, before handling papers and photographs to prevent leaving smudge marks and fingerprints.

Signs of Damage

- ❖ Documents with brown to black-colored stains and discolorations.
- ❖ Documents and photographs which have smudge marks or fingerprints.
- ❖ Photographic images which are obscured by dark-colored stains and discolorations.
- ❖ Documents and photographs covered with dust, dirt or soot.

Preventative Measures and Treatment

- ❖ Use an air purifier to cleanse the air of pollutants.
- ❖ Vacuum your storage area on a biweekly basis to reduce the accumulation of dust and other solid particles.
- ❖ Use a soft-haired brush to gently remove dust, dirt and soot from documents and photographs.
- ❖ Wash your hands before handling papers and photographs, or use latex or cotton gloves to prevent leaving smudge marks and fingerprints.

Water Damage

Documents and photographs which have incurred substantial *water damage* will require the services of a conservator. However, in the interim, the following measures should be followed to minimize further damage:

The stains on this photograph are a result of water damage caused by a flooded basement. (courtesy of Darren Kall and Lisa Purcell)

- ❖ Place water-soaked documents and photographs in an air-conditioned room that has a temperature at or below 65 degrees Fahrenheit to inhibit fungal growth.
- ❖ Use dehumidifiers and fans to facilitate the drying process and to maintain a constant flow of air.
- ❖ Carefully separate water-soaked items and place them on a flat surface between layers of highly absorbent fabric.
- ❖ Place a flat object such as a book on top of drying papers to minimize curling and wrinkling.

To protect against water damage, do not store your materials near water pipes, air conditioner units, radiators, windows, under skylights or directly against exterior walls. In addition, papers and photographs should be placed in a cabinet or another storage unit that is at least one foot above the floor to protect against possible flooding. Lastly, keep the following supplies on hand: plastic drop cloths, sponges, paper towels or highly absorbent fabric and buckets.

Signs of Damage

- ❖ Documents and photographs with water stains.
- ❖ Documents and photographs which have curled or wrinkled.
- ❖ Photographic emulsions which have loosened or separated from their support.

Preventative Measures and Treatment

- ❖ Do not place papers and photographs near water pipes, air conditioner units, radiators, windows, under skylights or directly against exterior walls.
- ❖ Store papers and photographs at least one foot above the floor to protect against possible flooding.
- ❖ Never use an iron to smooth wrinkled papers and photographs.

Framing

Framing documents and photographs for display in the home or office is an acceptable practice provided that the guidelines below are followed:

- ❖ Use frames made of aluminum or stainless steel. Wood, frames contain acidic compounds which will migrate to the framed item.
- ❖ Use Tru-Vu or Plexiglas rather than ordinary glass. Both filter out 93% of ultraviolet light.
- ❖ Use pH-balanced ragboard mats to protect the framed item from acid migration. Mats also prevent the item from direct contact with the glass, which protects the item against fungal and water damage caused by condensation on the glass. In addition, mats prevent the item from adhering to the glass surface.
- ❖ Secure the item to the mat with rag fiber hinges which have a pH-balanced adhesive. *Never use pressure-sensitive tape or commercial glues to secure the item.*
- ❖ Seal the back of the frame with pH-balanced backing paper to inhibit the accumulation of dust and insect infes-

tation. *Do not use cardboard or wood, which contain acidic compounds that will migrate to the framed item.*

- Once framed, the item should be situated in the room in such a way as to avoid direct exposure from sun and fluorescent light.

Signs of Damage

- Mat, backing paper and documents which are yellow to dark brown in color and that are brittle.
- Documents and photographs which have adhered to the glass surface.
- Documents and photographs which exhibit fungal growth.
- Documents and photographs which show signs of insect infestation.

Preventative Measures and Treatment

- Use aluminum or stainless-steel frames.
- Use plexiglass to protect the framed item from ultraviolet radiation.
- Use pH-balanced mats, backing paper and hinges to frame documents and photographs.
- Place the framed item in an area of a room where it will not be exposed to direct sun or fluorescent light.

Lamination

Lamination involves placing a document between two sheets of plastic which seals the item through the application of direct, intense heat or the use of a strong adhesive. Although lamination protects items from certain types of environmental damage, it is an inherently destructive process. Consequently, lamination should never be used to preserve papers or photographs for the following reasons:

- Lamination uses heat and adhesives which bond with the chemicals in paper and photographs to produce acidic compounds which cause the item to deteriorate.

- The plastic is chemically unstable and will eventually breakdown to form highly destructive acids.
- *The process is irreversible.* Once a document or photograph has been laminated, it is almost impossible to reverse the process without destroying the item.

Signs of Damage

- Documents and photographs which are yellow to dark brown in color.
- Cracked or yellowed plastic.

Preventative Measures and Treatment

- *Never laminate documents or photographs.*

Mechanical Disfigurement

This type of damage refers to the tears, perforations and stains caused by the use of *paper clips*, *staples*, *rubber bands*, *string* and *adhesives*, such as pressure-sensitive tape and commercial glues. These fasteners physically damage paper and photographs while the acidic chemical compounds contained in commercial adhesives and tape accelerate the deterioration of these materials. For example:

Under conditions of high relative humidity:

- *Metallic paper clips* and *staples* will oxidize (rust), which leaves reddish-brown stains.
- *Commercial adhesives*, such as rubber cement, will soften and leave brown-colored stains.
- *Rubber bands* will soften and adhere to paper and photographs.
- *Pressure-sensitive tape* will soften, lose its plastic support and leave permanent, sticky, brown-colored stains. Improper attempts at its removal will "skin" or tear the paper.
- *String* will become acidic and leave brown-colored lines on paper and photographs.

Under conditions of low relative humidity:

- ❖ *Rubber bands* will dry out and leave a hard, dark brown residue that adheres to paper and photographs.
- ❖ *Pressure-sensitive tape* will dry out, lose its adherence and leave a permanent, translucent or brown-colored residue.
- ❖ *Commercial adhesives* will dry out, lose their adherence and leave brown-colored stains.

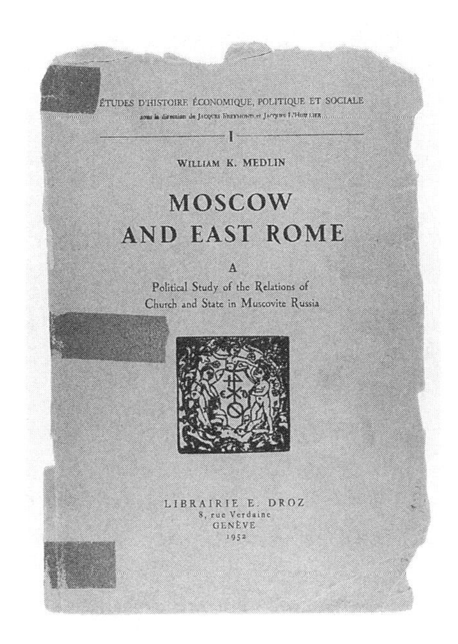
ÉTUDES D'HISTOIRE ÉCONOMIQUE, POLITIQUE ET SOCIALE

I

WILLIAM K. MEDLIN

MOSCOW
AND EAST ROME

A
Political Study of the Relations of
Church and State in Muscovite Russia

LIBRAIRIE E. DROZ
8, rue Verdaine
GENÈVE
1952

The cover of this book was repaired with pressure-sensitive tape, which has left permanent, brown-colored stains. (courtesy of the author)

For these reasons, *the above-mentioned fasteners and adhesives should never be used to attach or mend documents and photographs.* Staples, paper clips, rubber bands and string should be carefully removed from documents and replaced with *plastiklips,* which are made of a chemically stable plastic (see the chapter, "How to Perform Simple Repair and Cleaning"). Stainless steel paper clips may also be used but are more likely to cause perforations. *Plastiklips, however, should not be used to attach photographs* because they can scratch, crack and bend their emulsions. Torn documents and photographs should be mended with an archival-quality tape, which is pH-balanced and can be easily removed without causing damage to the item. Furthermore, when mending photographs always apply the tape to their paper side; *never apply archival tape to the emulsion.*

Signs of Damage

- ❖ Documents and photographs with tears, perforations and indentations.
- ❖ Documents and photographs encrusted with a hard, dark brown residue.
- ❖ Documents and photographs with hard-lined, translucent or brown-colored stains.

Preventative Measures and Treatment

- ❖ Replace paper clips and staples with chemically stable plastiklips.
- ❖ *Do not use rubber bands or string to bind papers or photographs.*
- ❖ Use pH-balanced archival-quality repair tape to mend torn documents and photographs. When mending photographs, be sure that the tape is placed on its paper side. *Never place tape on the emulsion.*
- ❖ Follow the instructions in the chapter, "How to Perform Simple Repair and Cleaning" to remove staples, paper clips, rubber bands and string.

Fire and Theft

The devastating impact of *fire* on paper and photographs is self-explanatory. However, this type of damage can usually be prevented by implementing the measures below:

- ❖ Install smoke alarms in key areas of your home. These alarms are excellent for early detection of fire.
- ❖ Store valuable documents in fire-resistant safes or a safe deposit box.
- ❖ Do not store papers, photographs and books near a fireplace, stove or radiator.
- ❖ Contact your local fire department for additional information on protecting your home from fire.

While *theft* is an unfortunate fact of life, the following measures can help to protect against the loss of your materials:

- ❖ Do not discuss the monetary value of your possessions with strangers.
- ❖ If you own items that are particularly valuable, install a security system.
- ❖ Insure valuable items and keep a list along with a photograph of each item in a safe deposit box. New items should be added to the list as they are acquired.
- ❖ Stolen books, documents, autographs or other items should be reported immediately to the police. If the value of the item(s) exceeds $5,000, also notify the Federal Bureau of Investigation. In addition, contact the Antiquarian Booksellers Association of America and American Book Prices Current. These organizations provide a service that will notify dealers and libraries of stolen items throughout the United States and Canada.

Chapter Five

How to Create a Friendly ENVIRONMENT

Introduction

As we have seen, environment is a principal factor in the preservation of paper and photographs that can either enhance the longevity of these materials or be the instrument of their destruction. This section provides step-by-step instructions to establish an environment that will help ensure the preservation of papers and photographs.

First Step: Selecting a Storage Room

Select a room that has a consistently moderate temperature and relative humidity. Do not use attics, basements or garages, which are subject to climate extremes, insect/rodent infestation and pollutants. The storage room should be free of household cleaners, paints and solvents, all of which emit destructive fumes. In addition, store documents and photographs in an area of the room that will provide maximum protection from potential water damage, sunlight and excessive temperatures. Lastly, *do not* store documents and photographs near the following: radiators, fireplaces, stoves, air conditioner units, pipes, windows, under skylights or against exterior walls.

Second Step: Setting Climate Controls

Once a storage room has been selected, set the thermostat to one of the two temperature/relative humidity ranges below. The level of relative humidity of the room can be determined by the use of Humidity Indicator cards. These cards contain chemicals which change color to indicate whether the conditions are dry, normal or humid.

If the conditions indicate a high level of humidity, use a dehumidifier to reduce the relative humidity. Conversely, if the conditions are excessively dry, a humidifier should be used to increase the level of humidity. Once these measures have been taken, use another humidity card to determine whether the conditions have reached a normal level. In addition, silica gel canisters should be placed near, but not in direct contact with, documents and photographs to absorb potential excess moisture.

Recommended Ranges of Temperature and Relative Humidity:

Optimal:

❖ Temperature: 65-68 degrees Fahrenheit
❖ Relative Humidity: 45-50 percent

Acceptable:

❖ Temperature: 69-71 degrees Fahrenheit
❖ Relative Humidity: 51-55 percent

Third Step: Maintaining a Constant Circulation of Air

Stagnant air enables fungal spores to settle on documents and photographs which causes the growth of mold and other fungi. Therefore, it is important to use fans to maintain a constant circulation of air in your storage room. In addition, an air purifier is strongly recommended to cleanse the air of pollutants and solid particles.

Fourth Step: Preventing Insect & Rodent Infestation

Thoroughly inspect documents and photographs for signs of insect or rodent infestation. If present, isolate the infested items to prevent further contamination, and then contact an exterminator or spray the infected areas with insecticides. *Be sure that the insecticides do not come into direct contact with your materials.* In addition, periodically check for any signs of re-infestation.

Fifth Step: Regulating Light Exposure

The deteriorative effects of light on documents and photographs can be reduced by minimizing its exposure to these materials as much as possible. The following measures should also be taken to regulate the amount of light to your storage room: use venetian blinds or curtains to restrict sun light, and place ultraviolet filters on windows and fluorescent lights to eliminate ultraviolet radiation. In addition, use low-watt incandescent bulbs, e.g. 60 watts, which emit lower levels of ultraviolet radiation than fluorescent lights. Be sure to place these bulbs at least four feet from your materials.

Chapter Six

How to Provide

Storage and Care

Introduction

The storage and care of paper and photographs are important factors in their preservation. Storage products such as file folders, envelopes and boxes help to protect documents and photographs from various types of damage caused by adverse environmental conditions as will the proper care of these materials. This chapter describes the proper storage, care and handling of paper-based and photographic materials.

Papers

Documents should first be placed in pH-balanced file folders, and then stored in document boxes which are pH-balanced, lignin-free and contain a buffer of calcium carbonate to retard acid migration. The use of these storage boxes is strongly recommended to help protect documents from the damaging effects of fungi, pollutants and light. Acidic documents (that are yellow to brown in color and brittle to the touch) should be interleaved with pH-balanced, buffered tissue paper or placed in a separate storage box to prevent acid migration to non-acidic documents. *Do not use commercial file folders and storage boxes which contain acidic chemical compounds which will accelerate paper deterioration.*

Oversized documents such as maps, blueprints, posters, etc., should be interleaved with pH-balanced, buffered tissue paper and then stored in flat file boxes or map cases. Be sure to note the contents of each box to facilitate retrieval. *Never fold or roll oversized documents*; both of these methods cause severe physical stress that will damage the document.

Be sure that your hands are clean before handling documents, and avoid handling documents in a rough manner, which can cause creases or tears. Before moving oversized documents, place them on a sheet of blotter paper that will support the item as it is being carried to its new location. In addition, use plastiklips to attach documents. *Do not use paper clips, staples, rubber bands, or string*; all of these will cause perforations and tears.

Drawings, Lithographs and Other Prints

Unframed works of art should always be handled with clean hands, or latex or cotton gloves should be used to prevent leaving smudge marks or fingerprints on their surfaces. To store these materials, cover the face of each item with buffered tissue paper and then place them in a pH-balanced, lignin-free flat file box. Number the box and then list the contents of the box on a separate sheet of paper.

Scrapbooks

Scrapbooks which contain acidic documents and photographs should be interleaved with buffered tissue paper cut to fit the size of the page, which will help to protect against acid migration. In addition, store scrapbooks in pH-balanced, lignin-free flat file boxes to protect them from light, pollutants and fungi.

Before starting a scrapbook, purchase an album made from pH-balanced materials; the pages should also be white or off-white in color to prevent color bleeding. Use pH-balanced paper or plastic mounts with a chemically stable adhesive to secure items on the pages. An acceptable, but less desirable, alternative to these mounts are pH-balanced hinges and the application of methyl cellulose, a pH-balanced adhesive. Oversized items such as newspaper or magazine clippings should be cut rather than folded to fit the size of the page.

Books

The proper storage, care and handling of books is an important factor in their preservation. Book cabinets and shelves should be located in an area of a room away from radiators, heating/water pipes, skylights and windows. Store books on shelves which have enough space to allow for their easy retrieval and replacement. In addition, keep one to two inches of space open at the top and back of the largest book to permit the air to circulate. Valuable and/or fragile books should be wrapped in buffered tissue paper, or they should be placed in pH-balanced, lignin-free slipcases or boxes, and then laid flat on a shelf.

The guidelines below provide additional recommendations for the care and handling of books:

- *Do not leave a book open flat or place it face down.* Both of these actions will cause the spine of the book to crack.
- When removing or replacing a book, grasp it by the middle of its sides, never by the top of its spine.
- *Do not place more than a three or four books on top of one another.*
- Use bookmarks rather than paper clips or folding ("dog-earing") pages.
- If bookplates are used, be sure that they contain a pH-balanced adhesive.
- Use a soft-haired brush to dust the edges and covers of a book.
- Use lanolin to clean leather book covers. Afterward, treat the book with a leather restorer/preservative using a lint-free cloth.
- Tie loose or separated books covers with unbleached, nonadhesive cloth strips.
- Use archival-quality tape to mend torn pages.

Comic Books, Journals and Magazines

These publications should be handled with clean hands, or wear latex or cotton gloves, to prevent leaving smudge marks or fingerprints. In addition, exercise care when handling these materials to prevent tears and creases to their covers and pages. Comic books are especially vulnerable to this type of damage due to the poor quality of the paper used in their production.

Solid particles such as dust, dirt and soot can be removed from these materials by using a soft-haired brush. *Do not use cloth rags or paper towels*, which will abrade the surface of the paper. Torn pages and covers should be mended with archival-quality tape. *Do not use pressure-sensitive tape*, which will damage the paper and leave hard-lined, brown-colored stains. To store these materials, use polyester (mylar) or polyethylene bags and then place them vertically in pH-balanced, lignin-free boxes using pH-balanced cardboard dividers as a support. Be sure to number each box and list its contents on a sheet of paper.

Stamps

When handling stamps, use a pair of tweezers to prevent tears and creases. Stamps should be placed in an album made of pH-balanced materials and whose pages are white or off-white in color to prevent color bleeding. In addition, use pH-balanced paper hinges with a chemically stable adhesive when placing stamps on a page. *Do not use pressure-sensitive tape or commercial adhesives*, both of which contain acids which will damage stamps.

Sports, Greeting and Postcards

These cards should be handled with clean hands, or wear latex or cotton gloves to prevent leaving smudge marks and fingerprints. Use archival-quality tape to mend torn cards by placing the tape on the non-image side of the card. *Never use pressure-tape to mend torn cards*. These cards may be placed in either pH-balanced paper or plastic enclosures to protect them from abrasion, pollutants and light. Polyester plastic enclosures are preferable because they allow for easy viewing and will reduce wear-and-tear of the item. Once they have been inserted in either paper or plastic enclosures, these cards should be stored vertically in pH-balanced, lignin-free boxes. Be sure to note the contents of each box on a sheet of paper.

Photographic Materials

Photographic prints should be placed in either pH-balanced photograph albums, pH-balanced paper or chemically stable plastic enclosures. The paper in photograph albums should also be white or off-white in color to prevent color bleeding. To secure photographs on album pages, use pH-balanced paper or plastic mounts that have a chemically stable adhesive. *Never use commercial adhesives*, which are acidic and will discolor photographs. pH-balanced paper envelopes may also be used to store photographs and negatives. Afterward, place the items in pH-balanced, lignin-free flat file boxes for additional protection.

Plastic enclosures may also be used to store photographs, negatives and transparencies. These enclosures should be made from chemically stable polyester, polypropylene or, polyethylene plastic. *Never use plastic enclosures made of polyvinyl chloride (PVC)*, which secretes hydrochloric acid that severely damages photographic emulsions. Magnetic photo albums should also be avoided because the paper, adhesives and plastic covers contain acidic chemical compounds. Interleave oversized photographs in pH-balanced, buffered tissue paper and then store them in pH-balanced, lignin-free flat file boxes (see "Photographic Materials with Special Care and Storage Needs" for information on photographs which should not be interleaved in buffered tissue paper). *Never roll oversized photographs*; this places enormous physical stress that will damage their emulsions. Lastly, when handling photographs, negatives, transparencies and movie film, be sure to hold them by their edges to avoid leaving fingerprints and smudge marks that will damage their emulsions.

Negatives can be placed in polyester, polypropylene or polyethylene plastic, or pH-balanced paper enclosures, and then stored in pH-balanced, lignin-free boxes. These enclosures will protect negatives from abrasion, pollutants and humidity and are available in a wide range of sizes. There are also various types of enclosures for transparencies that range from individual polypropylene sleeves to slide pages. Both types of enclosures permit easy viewing and help to protect emulsions from pollutants and excessive handling. In addition, there are a variety of storage containers for transparencies such as pH-balanced boxes, metal containers and two- to five-drawer metal cabinets.

Movie film that has been stored in metal containers should be removed and placed in pH-balanced, lignin-free storage boxes. In addition, use pH-balanced ID tags, instead of rubber bands or pressure-sensitive tape, to keep film wound on the reel. These tags also have a space to note the contents of the film.

Photographic Materials with Special Care and Storage Needs

The list below describes the special care and storage needs of the following photographic materials:

- *Daguerreotypes, Collodion and Albumen Photographic Materials* — Ambrotypes and daguerreotypes should be wrapped in non-buffered tissue paper and laid flat in a appropriate-sized, pH-balanced, lignin-free storage box. Albumen and tintype photographs should be placed in pH-balanced, non-buffered paper envelopes and then stored in pH-balanced, lignin-free storage boxes. *Buffered tissue paper should never be used for these photographic formats because it contains an alkaline substance that can damage their emulsions.*
- *Collodion and Dry Gelatin Glass Plate Negatives* — These negatives are easily damaged and, therefore, should be handled with great care. Use latex or cotton gloves when handling these negatives to prevent leaving fingerprints or smudge marks on their emulsions. Glass plate negatives should be placed in pH-balanced paper enclosures and then stored vertically in boxes fitted with grooved inserts to securely hold each negative in place. In addition, arrange the negatives by size to allow an even distribution of weight. Never stack glass plate negatives on top of one another; this will scratch their emulsions and cause the negatives toward the bottom to crack or break.

  Glass negatives which are cracked, chipped or broken should be wrapped in buffered tissue paper, placed between two pieces of sturdy, pH-balanced board cut to match the size of the negative, and then tied with strips of unbleached cotton cloth. Negatives which are cracked, broken or that have incurred other types of damage should be copied as soon as possible. Due to the fragile nature of glass plate negatives, it is strongly recommended that undamaged as well as damaged negatives be copied.

❖ *Color Negatives and Photographs* — these materials should be placed in pH-balanced, non-buffered paper envelopes or polyester, polypropylene or polyethylene plastic enclosures.

Chapter Seven

How to Perform Simple
REPAIR AND CLEANING

Introduction

As a rule, the conservation of papers and photographs should only be performed by a qualified conservator. However, there are some basic methods for cleaning and repairing documents and photographs which can safely be performed by the layperson. This chapter describes techniques for removing fasteners, cleaning documents and photographs, and performing simple repairs. There are also detailed instructions for deacidifying and encapsulating documents. Exercise good judgment and take your time when performing these techniques. In addition, *never attempt to repair or clean fragile documents and photographs*. These items should be treated by a conservator. Lastly, if you are uncomfortable or unsure about performing any of these techniques then it is best to leave the work to a conservator.

Removing Fasteners on Documents

The instructions below describe techniques for the removal of fasteners:

❖ *Staples* — The removal of staples will require the use of a microspatula. Turn the document to the side where the staple prongs are exposed using your other hand to support the paper. Slip the narrow end of the microspatula under one prong and bend it upward until it is vertical to the paper; repeat this action with the other prong. Turn the document over, slip the microspatula underneath the back of the staple and carefully lift it out. *Do not use staple removers*, which can cause tears to documents.

- ❖ *Paper Clips* — Hold the paper clip with one hand and with your other hand carefully lift the other end of the paper clip until it is vertical to the paper and can easily be removed.
- ❖ *Rubber Bands* — The removal of rubber band residue will also require the use of a microspatula. This procedure should be performed with great care and only on items that are in good condition. *Fragile documents and photographs should be treated by a conservator.*

  Place the document on a clean, flat surface. Hold the document with a moderate amount of pressure and use the microspatula to gently scrape off the residue a small portion at a time. *Never insert the microspatula between the residue and the paper*; this can cause tears or perforations to the paper. Note: *Rubber band residue on photographic emulsions should only be removed by a conservator.*

  To remove rubber bands that are soft and sticky, place the document on a clean, flat surface. Hold the document in place with two flat, moderately heavy objects on both ends of the paper. Gently lift one end of the rubber band with one hand and with the other hand insert the microspatula between the paper and the rubber band. Once this has been done, slowly move the microspatula in a cutting action to remove the rubber band.
- ❖ *String* — Use a pair of small scissors to cut the string and then carefully remove it from the item to prevent tears.
- ❖ *Pressure-sensitive Tape and Adhesives — The removal of tape and adhesives is an extremely delicate procedure that should only be performed by a conservator.*

Repairing Documents

- *Torn Documents* — Documents with tears can be mended with archival-quality tape. Use a pair of scissors to cut small strips of the tape and apply it sparingly to the torn areas. *Never use pressure-sensitive tape*, which can severely damage the document.
- *Folded Documents* — This technique should only be used on documents that are in good condition. *Fragile documents that are folded should be treated by a conservator.* To unfold a document, place it on a clean flat surface, slowly unfold, and then use a bone knife to gently smooth the creases. Afterward, insert the flattened item between two sheets of pH-balanced paper, and then place a moderately heavy, flat object on top of the item(s) for one or two weeks to keep it (them) flat.

Cleaning Documents

Documents can be cleaned by using a cleaning pad that gently removes surface dirt. However, *this pad should not be used on fragile documents or photographic materials.* To clean a document, squeeze the pad to allow the powder to fall on the soiled area(s) of the document. Gently rub the powder on the affected area and then remove the residue with a soft-haired brush. *Do not use commercial erasers*, which are highly abrasive, to clean documents.

Deacidification of Documents

Deacidification is a long-lasting treatment that uses a nontoxic, alkaline solution to neutralize the acids in paper and prevent the reoccurrence of acidity. However, this treatment will not reverse the damage caused by acids prior to its application. Deacidification solutions, such as Bookkeeper and Wei T'o, can be purchased as a liquid solution or an aerosol spray. Wei T'o is available in three different strengths. Use of the Number 2 solution or Number 10 spray is strongly recommended to deacidify documents because they both contain a mild alkaline. The No. 3 solution and No. 11 spray contain a stronger alkaline, for deeper penetration, which is intended for thicker paper and stable inks, No. 4 solution and No. 12 spray contain a powerful alkaline that should only be used for very thick papers and very stable inks.

The application of a deacidification solution should be performed in a well-ventilated room that has an exhaust fan to ensure that the fumes are eliminated from the work area. Before treating the document, it is recommended that the solution be tested on a small area of the document using a cotton swab or a small brush. If there is no adverse effect to either the paper or the ink, then the solution may be applied to the rest of the document. Carefully follow the guidelines below:

- ❖ Pour a small amount of the solution into a small glass container, such as a baby-food jar.
- ❖ Apply the solution to the document using a medium- to large-sized, soft-haired brush.
- ❖ Apply the solution in even strokes.
- ❖ Once the solution has dried, use a soft-haired dust brush to remove the white powder residue.
- ❖ Pour any remaining solution back into the bottle for future use. BE SURE TO KEEP THE SOLUTION OUT OF THE REACH OF CHILDREN!

Non-acidic documents may also be deacidified to protect them from future occurrences of acidity. However, due to the high cost of deacidification solution, it is wise to evaluate the importance and condition of documents before undertaking this treatment.

Important: *Never apply deacidification solution to photographs.*

Encapsulation of Documents

This technique is used to enclose a document between two sheets of polyester plastic (a chemically stable plastic with a neutral pH) that is sealed on all four sides with double-sided, pH-balanced tape. Encapsulation protects the enclosed item from the damage caused by pollutants, fungi and excessive handling. In addition, this technique can easily be undone without damaging the enclosed document.

Since the cost of polyester plastic (mylar) tends to be expensive, assess the importance and the condition of the items before they are encapsulated. If there are a large number of documents to be encapsulated, it is more economical to purchase a roll of mylar than individual pre-cut sheets. Both polyester rolls and pre-cut sheets are available in five thicknesses: Mil 1 (lowest) through Mil 5 (highest), and a variety of sizes. Lastly, before encapsulating a document, practice the technique using blank sheets of paper until it has been perfected.

To encapsulate a document, carefully follow the instructions below:

- Use two sheets of mylar whose dimensions are one inch (1") larger than the document to be encapsulated.
- Place the document on the bottom sheet and use a moderately heavy object to hold the document in place.
- Apply the double-sided tape to the four edges of the mylar sheet. Be sure to leave a space measuring one quarter (1/4") to one half (1/2") inch between the tape and the edge of the document.
- Once the tape is in place, peel away its paper backing and remove the object on top of the document.
- Carefully place the top sheet so that it is properly aligned to the bottom sheet.
- Use a soft tissue and apply moderate pressure to the top sheet along the strips of tape to seal the document.
- Trim the pointed edges of the plastic with a scissor.

Important: *Charcoal, graphite and pastel drawings should* ***not*** *be encapsulated. Polyester plastic carries a static charge that can loosen or remove these pigments.*

Repairing Photographs

- *Torn Photographs* — Use archival-quality tape to mend torn photographs by placing the tape on the paper side of the photograph. *Never apply tape to the emulsion, negatives or transparencies.* Daguerreotypes, ambrotypes, and tintypes that have been damaged should be treated by a conservator.

- ❖ *Curled Photographs* — Photographs which are in good condition and exhibit a minimal amount of curling can be flattened by following the instructions below. However, *do not use this procedure on old, fragile or rolled photographs*. These items should be treated by a conservator. The sponge and blotter paper mentioned below can be purchased at a photographic supply store.

Follow the guidelines below to uncurl photographs:

- ❖ Lightly moisten the back of the photograph with a pH-balanced sponge.
- ❖ Place the photograph between two sheets of pH-balanced blotter paper.
- ❖ Place a moderately heavy object on top of the blotter paper for a few days.

Cleaning Photographs

Use a non-water-based photograph cleaner to remove finger oils, ball-point inks, adhesives and soot from photographs, negatives and transparencies. However, *do not use this solution on daguerreotypes, ambrotypes, tintypes, or glass plate negatives*. The cleaning of these materials should be performed by a conservator.

Chapter Eight

Paper and Photograph ARRANGEMENT

Introduction

Everyone, at one time or another, has experienced the frustration of trying to locate a particular document among a stack of papers. This situation is not only frustrating but often results in tears, creases and excessive wear to papers and photographs. On the other hand, paper and photograph collections which are well organized reduce the wear-and-tear to these materials and facilitate their retrieval. This chapter describes the basic principals of document and photograph arrangement.

Before undertaking the arrangement of your papers, it is important to thoroughly review the documents to determine if an arrangement already exists. If there is a discernible arrangement, then it should be kept because it is much easier to maintain an existing arrangement than to establish a new one. Moreover, by maintaining the original arrangement, additional insight can be gained regarding the person or persons who created the collection. If, however, the collection does not have a discernible arrangement, then one should be established.

Papers: Levels of Arrangement

Collection

A *collection* is a term used to describe a body of documents that have a common relationship. The nature of this relationship can be based on a person, family, organization, subject or event. The collection has a hierarchical, pyramid-like structure within which documents are arranged into related groups which become more specific at each succeeding level. The division of documents is based on their informational content, such as a particular subject, person, family, function, or by type of document.

The diagram below illustrates the pyramid-type structure that should be used to arrange documents.

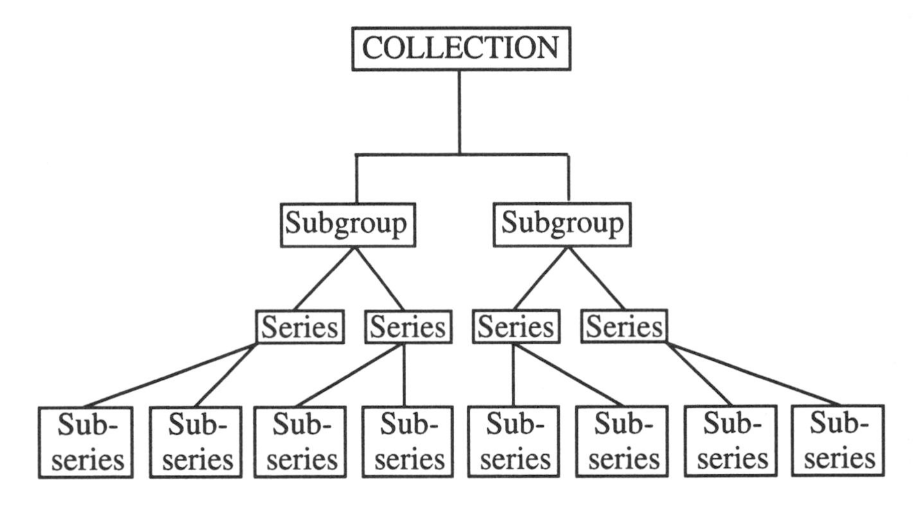

Subgroup

The *subgroup* level of arrangement divides documents within a collection into broad, related groups by function or person(s). In the case of personal papers, subgroups are usually arranged by function, such as the person's job, interests, volunteer activities, etc. The following example illustrates the use of subgroups based on function for a collection of personal papers:

Collection: William Anderson Papers

Subgroup: Vice-President, Southeast Widgets, Inc.
Subgroup: President, Model Shipbuilding Club
Subgroup: Volunteer Director, American Red Cross

Family papers should be organized into subgroups if the activities of individual members are distinct from those of the family as a whole. Family papers which do not reflect such groups should be arranged on the *series* level (see below). The following example illustrates the use of subgroups for the Thompson Family Papers:

Collection: Thompson Family Papers

Subgroup: Mary Thompson
Subgroup: Peter Thompson
Subgroup: Samuel Thompson
Subgroup: Thompson Family

The above-mentioned subgroups for Mary, Peter and Samuel Thompson contain documents which relate specifically to their business and social activities, while the Thompson Family subgroup consists of documents that relate to activities in which Mary, Peter and Samuel *all* took part. However, it may be preferable to organize the papers of individual family members as a separate collection.

Series

The *series* is the next level of arrangement in which documents are organized by the following: type of document, subject and event. The following example illustrates the use of series in the arrangement of documents within the subgroups: Mary Thompson and the Thompson Family.

Sub-Group: Mary Thompson

Series: Correspondence (type of document)
Series: Financial Documents (type of document)
Series: Legal Documents (type of document)
Series: Williams Mining Company (subject)

Sub-Group: Thompson Family

Series: General Correspondence (type of document)
Series: Family Reunion (event)

At the series level, an arrangement by type of document is a simple but effective means of arrangement because the format of a document can easily be determined. However, a type of document arrangement should not be used if the documents are better suited to an arrangement by subject or event.

Sub-series

The *sub-series* is the next level of arrangement whereby documents are further divided into related groups, within in the series, based on the following criterion: type of document, subject and event. At this level of arrangement, it is also important to note the inclusive dates (earliest date to the last date) of the documents contained within the sub-series. The example below illustrates the use of the sub-series:

Collection: Thompson Family Papers

Subgroup: Mary Thompson

Series: Correspondence (type of document)

Sub-series: Greeting Cards - July, 1941-May, 1943 (type of document)
Sub-series: Letters - August, 1942-April, 1944 (type of document)
Sub-series: Telegrams - June, 1944-March, 1946 (type of document)

Series: Financial Documents (type of document)

Sub-series: Bank Statements - July, 1942-November, 1943 (type of document)
Sub-series: Receipts - May, 1939-September, 1941 (type of document)

Series: Legal Documents (type of document)

Sub-series: Insurance Policy - Acme Insurance - March, 1951 (type of document)

Sub-series: Mortgage - Hampton Hills Property - August, 1939 (type of document)

Series: Printed Material (type of document)

Sub-series: Brochures - April, 1939-November, 1941 (type of document)
Sub-series: Newspaper Clippings - May, 1939-December, 1939 (type of document)

Series: Williams Mining Company (subject)

Sub-Series: Correspondence - January, 1948-August, 1950 (type of document)
Sub-Series: Board of Directors Minutes - June, 1939-May, 1940 (function)
Sub-Series: Miners' Strike - July, 1938 (subject)

When arranging document collections, be sure that the file folders list the series, sub-series and inclusive dates of the documents. The example below illustrates how a folder title should be written:

(Series) (Sub-series) (Date)
Legal Documents: Deed to Williams County Property — June, 1900

The document box that holds the folders should have a label listing the contents of the box by the collection, subgroup, series and inclusive dates of the documents. For example:

Thompson Family Papers (collection)
Peter Thompson (subgroup)
Financial Documents (series)
1901-1905 (inclusive dates)

Once your papers have been arranged and then placed in file folders and document boxes, it is important to write an inventory of the contents within each box to facilitate their retrieval. An example of a collection inventory is listed on the next page.

Thompson Family Papers

Box 1

Series: Correspondence

1. Greeting Cards - 1896-1899
2. Letters - April, 1898-January, 1899
3. Letters - May, 1900-July, 1901
4. Letters - December, 1901-February, 1903
5. Telegrams - March, 1897-June, 1898

Box 2

Series: Financial Documents

1. Bank Statements - January, 1920-July, 1922
2. Bills - March, 1919-September, 1922
3. Income Tax Returns - 1928-1930
4. Receipts - June, 1915-November, 1918

Box 3

Series: Legal Documents

1. Birth Certificates - 1900-1951
2. Death Certificates - 1896-1948
3. Marriage Certificates - 1888-1942
4. Mortgages - 1901-1956
5. Wills - 1908-1939

Box 4

Series: Literary Productions

1. Diaries - Aunt Mary - 1901-1912
2. Diaries - Uncle Joe - 1889-1901
3. Memoirs - Great Grandfather William - 1862
4. Speeches - "My Life As A Coal Miner" - Grandfather James - June, 1928

Box 5

Series: Printed Material

1. Diplomas - 1929-1956
2. Newspaper Clippings - June, 1902-December, 1906
3. Programs - February, 1899-April, 1903

Photographs

The content of photographs and the circumstances, i.e., the event, location, subject or person(s) depicted in the photographs, are the criteria which should be used to determine their arrangement. For example, photographs taken at weddings, birthday parties and family reunions should be organized by the event. Other types of photographs can be arranged by subject or location such as Horses (subject) or the Grand Canyon (location). Further, a general category is useful for organizing photographs of individuals in settings which cannot be identified. The following is a list of the categories in which photographs may be arranged:

- ❖ *Event* — weddings, birthdays, family reunions, bar mitzvahs, vacations, etc.
- ❖ *Location* — an identifiable landscape, citiscape, building, etc.
- ❖ *Subject* — photographs of cars, trains, animals, buildings, streets, landscapes which cannot be identified.
- ❖ *Portraits* — individual or group
- ❖ *General* — photographs of individuals in settings which cannot be identified.

Since most photographs can be arranged by more than one of the above-mentioned categories, it is important to determine the primary category by which to organize your photographs. This decision should be based on how meaningful the occasion was to you and whoever else was there when the photograph(s) were taken. For example, photographs taken of the Thompson Family Picnic at Hanging Rock could be organized by the event (Thompson Family Picnic) or location (Hanging Rock). However, the picnic (event) is probably more meaningful for the Thompson Family than where it was held, Hanging Rock (location); therefore, the photographs should be arranged by the event. Similarly, photographs taken at the Grand Canyon during a family vacation would be better arranged by the event (Vacation in Arizona) than by the location (Grand Canyon) because the photographs have a stronger association with the vacation than the location. However, let's say that during a routine business trip you stopped by to see the Grand Canyon and took some photographs. These photographs are more likely to have a stronger association with the location than the event and, therefore, should be arranged by location.

The identification of photographs is also important because, over time, the circumstances, the individuals and the dates of the photographs are frequently forgotten. Therefore, it is strongly recommended that information regarding the event, location, person(s) depicted and the date be noted on the back of each photograph using a No. 2 pencil or on a sheet of paper. If the latter is selected, number each photograph and write that number on the paper along with the pertinent data. For example, Wedding of William and Mary Edwards, July 8, 1983; Vacation at Disney World, February 19-26, 1986; John Campbell, June 4, 1979; or, George Fielding, David Newcastle, and Janet Thompson in front of the Empire State Building, November 7, 1965. In the case of duplicate photographs, a letter should be added to the number, e.g., 25A, 25B, etc.

Appendix A

Damage/Cause

Reference Guide

The guide below lists the types of damage to paper and photographs, the environmental cause and the page number for information.

Types of Damage	*Causes*	*Page*
Dry, brittle paper/photos	Temp/RH, Light	33, 38
Discolored paper/photos	Temp/RH, Light, Pollutants	33, 38, 40
Limp, easily torn paper	Temp/RH, Fungi	33, 35
Water stains	Temp/RH, Water Damage	33, 43
Adhered papers/photos	Temp/RH, Water Damage	33, 43
Inks that have run	Temp/RH, Water Damage	33, 43
Wrinkled photos	Temp/RH, Water Damage	33. 43
Cracked, marred photos	Temp/RH, Light	33, 38
Yellow-brown paper	Temp/RH, Light	33, 38
Faded text	Light	38
Metallic sheen on photos	Light	38

Types of Damage	*Causes*	*Page*
Faded photos	Light	38
Brown, fibrous spots	Fungi	35
Obscured photo/text	Fungi, Pollutants	35, 40
Dark, encrusted spots	Insects/Rodents	35
Holes, small to large	Insects/Rodents	35
Shredded paper	Rodents	36
Smudges/fingerprints	Pollutants	40
Dust, Dirt, Soot	Pollutants	40
Tears and holes	Mechanical Disfigurement	46
Hard, dark brown residue	Mechanical Disfigurement	46

Appendix B

Recommended

PRESERVATION SUPPLIES

Introduction

The preservation supplies listed below will be useful in the care and storage of documents and photographs. They have been organized into the following categories: Storage, Repair, Environmental Control and Miscellaneous. All of these supplies can be purchased through one or more of the preservation supply companies listed in Appendix C.

Storage

Archival-quality Albums — Composed of pH-balanced materials and buffered with calcium carbonate to retard acid migration, these albums can be used as scrapbooks or photograph albums. Album pages are available in pH-neutral polypropylene or polyester (mylar) plastic, or paper. White or off-white pages should be used to prevent color bleeding.

Boxes — These containers are pH-balanced, lignin-free and contain a buffer of calcium carbonate to retard acid migration. They are beneficial in organizing paper and photograph collections and will also protect these materials from humidity, pollutants and light. Storage boxes are available in a wide variety of sizes.

Enclosures — These materials are pH-balanced and will protect papers and photographs from the damaging effects of pollutants, humidity and excessive handling. They are available in the following formats: sleeves, envelopes, file folders, pre-cut and rolled sheets.

Repair

Archival-quality Repair Tape — This pH-neutral tape should be used sparingly to mend torn documents and book pages. If necessary, the tape can be removed without causing damage to the item.

Bone Knife — This instrument is made from animal bone and is useful for smoothing the creases in folded paper.

Cloth Tape — This product is useful for reattaching or reinforcing book covers. Use a non-bleached, cloth tape that contains a pH-balanced adhesive.

Deacidification Solution — This solution contains a weak alkaline solution that neutralizes the acids in paper, protects the document from future acid contamination and effectively extends the lifespan of the document. Recommended deacidification solutions are Bookkeeper and Wei T'o (available as a liquid solution or an aerosol spray and in three different strengths). It is strongly recommended that Wei T'o No. 2 liquid solution or No. 10 aerosol spray be used on documents. Be sure to test a small area of the document with a cotton swab or small brush before applying the solution. *Deacidification solution should never be used on photographs.*

Document Cleaning Pad — This pad removes surface dirt on documents but *should not be used on fragile documents or photographic materials.* Squeeze the pad to allow the powder to fall on the soiled area(s) of the document. Gently rub the powder on the affected area and then remove the residue with a soft-haired brush. *Never use commercial erasers on documents*, as they are highly abrasive.

Dusting Brush — This soft-bristled brush gently removes dust, dirt and soot from documents and photographs. It should be used instead of cloth rags or paper towels, which are abrasive.

Lanolin — This product cleans leather-bound books and should be used before applying leather restorer/preservative.

Leather Restorer and Preservative — This product is useful for the restoration and preservation of leather-bound books. It neutralizes acids and contains buffering agents that protect leather against the damaging effects of pollutants and fungi.

Microspatula — This instrument has two flattened ends, one narrow and the other rounded. It can be used to remove staples and the residue from rubber bands.

Photograph Cleaner — A non-water-based product, it removes finger oils, ball-point pen inks, adhesives, and soot from photographs, negatives and transparencies. Use a lint-free cloth or a cotton ball to apply the solution.

Unbleached Cloth Strips — These cloth strips are pH-balanced and free of dyes. They should be used to tie books whose covers have loosened or fallen off.

Environmental Control

Humidity Indicator Cards — These cards contain chemicals which change color to indicate whether the relative humidity is dry, normal or humid. They are an inexpensive means of checking the humidity levels in your storage room.

Silica Gel Canisters — These canisters absorb excess moisture and should be placed near, but not in direct contact with, documents and photographs.

Ultraviolet (UV) Light Filters — These filters are highly effective in filtering out the ultraviolet spectrum but will not interfere with the emission of visible light. They are available in sheets for use on windows and plastic tubes for fluorescent lights.

Miscellaneous

Cotton or Latex Gloves — These gloves are useful in preventing finger oils from leaving permanent marks or smudges on documents and photographs.

Framing Materials — Use pH-balanced mats, backboards, hinges and backing paper when framing documents and photographs. In addition, mats and backing paper should also contain a buffer of calcium carbonate to retard acid migration.

Mounting Corners — These items are useful for securing documents and photographs in scrapbooks. They are available in pH-neutral polypropylene plastic and buffered paper; both contain a self-sticking, pH-balanced adhesive.

Movie Film ID Tags — These pH-balanced tags are useful for identifying the contents of a film and have a pH-balanced adhesive strip that keeps the film tightly wound.

Plastiklips — Plastiklips are made of a chemically stable plastic and should be used instead of paper clips or staples. They are available in three sizes: small, medium and large.

Tissue Paper — This type of paper is pH-balanced and can be purchased with or without a buffer of calcium carbonate. Buffered tissue paper should be used to interleave documents and wrap most types of photographs. *Non-buffered* tissue should be used to wrap the following: daguerreotypes, collodion and albumen photographic materials.

Appendix C

Recommended
PRESERVATION PRODUCT SUPPLIERS

The preservation supply companies listed below offer a wide variety of products useful for the preservation of papers and photographs. Write, phone or fax to request a catalog. In addition, the *Museum and Archival Supplies Handbook* contains a comprehensive list of preservation supply companies in the United States and Canada. It is available for purchase through the Society of American Archivists (see Appendix D).

Archival Products, Inc.
2134 East Grand
P.O. Box 1413
Des Moines, IA 50305
Phone: 800-526-5640

Conservation Materials Ltd.
240 Freeport Boulevard
P.O. Box 2884
Sparks, NV 89432
Phone: 702-331-0582

Conservation Resources International, Inc.
8000-H Forbes Place
Springfield, VA 22151
Phone: 800-634-6932
Fax: 703-321-0629

Gaylord Bros.
Box 4901
Syracuse, NY 13221-4901
Phone: 800-448-6160 Fax: 800-272-3412

G.M. Wylie Company
P.O. Box AA
Washington, PA 15301-0660
Phone: 800-747-1249 Fax: 412-262-5254

Hollinger Corporation
9401 Northeast Drive/P.O. Box 8360
Fredericksburg, VA 22404
Phone: 800-634-0491 Fax: 800-947-8814

Light Impressions
439 Monroe Avenue/P.O. Box 940
Rochester, NY 14603-0940
Phone: 800-828-6216 Fax: 800-828-5539

The Preservation Emporium
2707 N. Stemmons Fwy. / Ste. 140
Dallas, TX 75207
Phone: 800-442-2038

Solar Screen
53-11 105th Street
Corona, NY 11368
Phone: 718-592-8222

TALAS
213 West 35th Street
New York, NY 10001
Phone: 212-736-7744

University Products
517 Main Street/P.O. Box 101
Holyoke, MA 01041-0101
Phone: 800-762-1165 Fax: 800-532-9281

The following companies sell hand- and cylinder-made paper that is acid-free and 100% cotton and linen rag. Some of these companies also sell a variety of related supplies such as framing materials, permanent inks and bookbinding supplies. Write or phone to request a catalog.

Carriage House Paper
79 Guernsey Street
Brooklyn, NY 11222
Phone: 800-669-8781

Daniel Smith Inc.
4150 First Avenue South
P.O. Box 84268
Seattle, WA 98124
Phone: 800-426-6740

Dieu Donne Papermill Inc.
433 Broome Street
New York, NY 10013
Phone: 212-226-0573

Paper Source
232 West Chicago Avenue
Chicago, IL 60610
Phone: 312-337-0798

Twinrocker Handmade Paper, Inc.
P. O. Box 413
Brookston, IN 47923
Phone: 800-757-TWIN

Appendix D

Sources for

ADDITIONAL INFORMATION

AB Bookman's Weekly
P.O. Box AB
Clifton, NJ 07015
Phone: 201-772-0020

This organization publishes a weekly magazine on topics relating to books, manuscripts and photographs, including the preservation of these materials. The magazine also has a Missing Book section and a listing of booksellers and conservators.

American Book Prices Current
Old Litchfield Road
Washington, CT 06793
Phone: 203-868-0080

This organization offers an on-line service called BAM-BAM that notifies dealers and libraries of stolen books, documents and autographs throughout the United States and Canada.

American Institute for Conservation of Historic
and Artistic Works
1717 "K" Street
Suite 301
Washington, DC 20006
Phone: 202-452-9545

The American Institute for Conservation can provide the name, address and phone number of a conservator in your area.

Antiquarian Booksellers Association of America
50 Rockefeller Plaza
New York, New York 10020
Phone: 212-757-9395

The ABAA offers a pamphlet titled *Rare Books and Manuscript Thefts: A Security System for Librarians, Booksellers and Collectors*, and a *Membership Directory of Book Dealers*. In addition, they have a service that notifies dealers and libraries of stolen books, documents and autographs.

Library of Congress
National Preservation Program
LMG-07
Washington, DC 20540
Phone: 202-707-1840

The National Preservation Program office provides information for water- and fire-damaged materials and the preservation of books.

National Archives
Washington, DC 20408
Phone: 202-523-3220

The National Archives provides information on paper and photograph preservation, genealogical and historical research.

Society of American Archivists
600 S. Federal, Suite 504
Chicago, IL 60605
Phone: 312-922-0140

The Society of American Archivists has an extensive list of publications, some of which relate to paper and photograph preservation. Write to request a copy of their publications catalog.

State, County and City Archives

These archives are listed in the government section of the telephone directory. Their staffs can provide information on paper and photograph preservation.

Preservation

GLOSSARY

Acids — Acids belong to a class of chemicals that have different strengths and properties but which all have a pH value of below 7.0. Acids will accelerate the deterioration of paper and photographs.

Acid-free — A term used for materials that have a pH value of 7.1 or higher.

Acid Migration — The transfer of acidity from one document or photograph to another either through physical contact or acidic vapors.

Alkalines — Alkalines belong to a class of chemicals that have different strengths and properties but which all have a pH value of 7.1 or higher. Alkalines are used to neutralize the acids in paper.

Archival-quality/Conservation-quality — Terms used to indicate that a material is chemically stable and, therefore, has a stronger resistance to adverse environmental conditions.

Calcium Carbonate — A colorless or white alkaline chemical that is used as a buffer in paper and storage boxes to inhibit the formation and migration of acids.

Cellulose — The principle component of wood and plants, cellulose is the fibrous material used in the manufacture of paper.

Chemical Pulping — A process that involves cooking wood fiber in a chemical solution to dissolve lignin and other wood-based impurities.

Chemical Stability — The ability of certain chemical bonds to resist changes in their composition when exposed to other chemicals. Paper and photographs which are chemically stable are more resistant to deterioration.

Conservation — The use of certain procedures, techniques and materials to chemically stabilize and physically strengthen paper and photographs.

Deacidification — A treatment used to neutralize the acids in paper by applying a mild alkaline solution. Deacidification, however, does not reverse the damage caused by acids prior to its application.

Encapsulation — A technique used to enclose an item between two sheets of polyester (mylar) plastic using double-sided, pH-balanced tape to seal all the edges. Encapsulation protects the item from pollutants, fungi and excessive handling. The technique can easily be undone without damage to the enclosed item.

Environment — The external influences which chemically alter the composition of paper and photographs and, thus, accelerate their deterioration.

Hygroscopic — The ability of a material such as paper or photographs to absorb or release moisture in response to the relative humidity.

Lamination — An inherently destructive process that reinforces paper through enclosure between two sheets of chemically unstable plastic by sealing it with heat or acidic adhesives.

Lignin — An organic bonding material found in wood fiber. The acidic properties of lignin have a deteriorative effect on paper and photographs.

Mechanical Pulping (Groundwood Pulp) — A process that involves grinding wood into short-length fibers. Mechanically pulped paper retains most of its wood-based impurities and processing chemicals and, therefore, tends to be weak and chemically unstable.

Methyl Cellulose — A pH-balanced powder that dissolves in water to form a nontoxic paste that can be used as an adhesive.

Paper Molds — Wooden frames fitted with tightly woven screens which are used to form individual sheets of paper.

pH Scale — A scale that uses numbers from 0 to 14 to measure the level of acidity or alkalinity in paper and photographs. Each number from 6.9 to 0 indicate tenfold increases in *acidity* while the numbers from 7.1 to 14 indicate the same increase in *alkalinity*. A pH level of 7 is neutral.

Polyester (Mylar) Plastic — A chemically stable, durable and transparent plastic that is used to encapsulate or enclose documents and photographic materials.

Polyethylene Plastic — A chemically stable, transparent plastic used to enclose documents and photographic materials.

Polypropylene Plastic — This type of plastic is chemically stable, resists heat and is stiffer than polyethylene. It is used to enclose documents and photographic materials.

Preservation — The various methods used to maintain paper, photographs and other materials in either their original form or by copying them onto another format such as microfilm.

Relative Humidity — The percentage of moisture in the air relative to the maximum amount the air can hold at that temperature.

Sizing — A process in the manufacture of paper that uses alum rosin or other chemicals to permit the application of ink.

Temperature — A standard measurement used to determine the degree of hotness or coldness in an environment.

Ultraviolet (UV) Radiation — A short wave light spectrum that alters the chemical composition of paper and photographs.

Bibliography

Clapp, Anne F., *Curatorial Care of Works of Art on Paper: Basic Procedures for Paper Preservation*, 4th ed. New York: Nick Lyons Books, 1987.

Dorin, Henry, *Modern Principles of Chemistry*. New York: Standard Publishing, 2nd ed. 1971

Greenfield, Jane, *The Care of Fine Books*. New York: Lyons and Burford, 1988.

Hunter, Dard, *Papermaking: The History and Technique of an Ancient Craft*. New York: Dover Publications, Inc., 1978

Pauling, Linus, *General Chemistry*. New York: Dover Publications, Inc., 1988.

Reilly, James M., *Care and Identification of 19th Century Photographic Prints*. Rochester, New York: Eastman Kodak Company, 1986.

Ritzenthaler, Mary Lynn, *Archives and Manuscripts: Conservation*. Chicago, Illinois: Society of American Archivists, 1983.

Ritzenthaler, Mary Lynn, Munoff, Gerald J., Long, Margery S., *Administration of Photographic Collections*. Chicago, Illinois: Society of American Archivists, 1984.

Studley, Vance, *The Art and Craft of Handmade Paper*. New York: Dover Publications, 1990.

Turner, Silvie, *Which Paper? A Guide to Choosing Fine Papers for Artists, Craftspeople, and Designers.* New York: Design Press, 1992.

Index

A

B

C

D

E

F

G

H

I

J

K

L

M

N

O

P

R

S

T

U

V

W

About the Author

Craig A. Tuttle

Craig Tuttle holds a B.A., M.A. in History and a Certificate in Archival Management from New York University. Mr. Tuttle has served as Project Archivist for the Fiorello LaGuardia Mayoral Papers, University Archivist for the University of South Florida, and as an archival consultant. He has also served as a member of the Mayor of Tampa's Archives Advisory Committee. Mr. Tuttle has frequently lectured on the preservation of papers and photographs and has been the subject of numerous newspaper and magazine articles.

An Ounce of Preservation
A Guide to the Care of Papers and Photographs
Craig A. Tuttle

Copies of *An Ounce of Preservation can* be had by

- ❖ calling, toll free, 1-800-356-9315, Visa/MC/Amex accepted.

- ❖ sending $12.95, plus $3.00 shipping and handling, plus applicable sales tax to Rainbow Books, Inc., P. O. Box 430, Highland City, FL 33846-0430, Telephone/Fax (941) 648-4420, Email: NAIP@aol.com.

- ❖ asking your bookseller for ISBNumber 1-56825-021-5

This entire page, as well as the cover of *An Ounce of Preservation*, can be modified to reflect your large-quantity, special purchase.

More information on the following types of purchases can be made directly to the Publisher, Betty Wright, at P. O. Box 430, Highland City, FL 33846-0430, Telcphonc/Fax (941) 648-4420, Email: NAIP@aol.com

Bulk
Nonprofit Corporate
Corporate Premium
Corporate Incentive
Fund-raiser
Employee Reward

What the experts say about *An Ounce of Preservation*

". . . a very valuable resource guide . . . wonderfully readable . . . crammed full of useful information in an easy-to-understand format . . . must-have reference guide . . . You may want to order two, one for yourself and one for your favorite genealogy society."

— Carole Kiernan,
"Family Heirlooms," *The Tri-City Record* (MI)

"This book, written with knowledge and enthusiasm, is an introduction for collectors and other non-archivists into preserving papers and photographs . . . a valuable reference for recognizing and treating deterioration and for understanding how to provide a friendly environment for your collections and family heirlooms."

— Helen B. Henderson,
"Book Review," *Maine Antique Digest*

" . . . Nearly everyone has a collection of papers and photographs, and require some type of storage for them. It may be that instead of preserving our collections, we are contributing to their deterioration."

— Sharon D. Warrix,
"Genealogy Notes," *Appalachian News-Express* (KY)

"Documents and photographs are commonly found among the treasures of family historians. Yet few of us know much about their care and preservation. Genealogists will want to add *An Ounce of Preservation* . . . to their personal libraries. A most enlightening and easy-to-read book . . . "

— Myra Gormley,
"Family Tree," *Seattle Post-Intelligencer,*
"Preserving Family Treasures," Prodigy

" . . . of interest to people in many different fields . . . Written in a simple, easy-to-read manner, Tuttle's guide shows how an ounce of preservation today can help to save for tomorrow paper and photographic materials that will otherwise be lost."

— Marleta Childs,
"Kin Searching," *Amarillo Globe News* (TX),
Jacksonville Daily Progress (FL)

" . . . valuable information for everyone . . ."

— *The Maine Genealogical Society Newsletter*

"For all searchers of and preservers of family history knowing some basics about preservation of paper and photograph heirlooms is certainly a must. In this brief, attractive volume aimed at the layman the author lays a background of understanding enough of the history of papermaking, chemistry of ink and the elements of photography for us to appreciate the nature of the items in our care . . . Do your descendants a favor by taking a look at the ideas in this little volume and perhaps lengthening the life of some of your family heirlooms."

— Genealogical Forum of Oregon, Inc.

"As we enter the home stretch of this holiday season [Christmas], millions of photographs will be snapped, and even more cards and letters will be mailed. Whether we are sentimental and save them all, or are efficient and save only the best, these relics embody our memories. How can we keep these mementos, as well as important documents, posters, books, baseball cards, and other paper and photo-based items safe from deterioration? Author Craig Tuttle, in his deceptively slim book . . . provides answers . . . more than just a how-to book of archival preservation. It is also a wonderful history lesson . . . a delight to read and easy to use . . . full of so many useful, easy-to-follow instructions that most readers will be able to take better care of their memories right away."

— Wendy Machaver,
"Protecting Our Memories," *Clinton Chronical*

"I like *An Ounce of Preservation: a guide to the care of papers and photographs* by Craig A. Tuttle, Rainbow Books, 1994. Also the Gaylord Preservation Pathfinder series. I've used both in classes for the public and local genealogical groups."

— anonymous blurb on the archivists listserv

" . . . Tuttle stresses prevention with common-sense suggestion — no exotic formulas, expensive chemicals and difficult-to-duplication solutions . . ."

— Carol Collins,
"Michiana Roots," *South Bend Tribune* (IN)

"Many genealogists are not satisfied to just get the charts done on their family history, but they also like to augment their written research with photographs, documents, letters, diaries and scrapbooks. For those of us who are interested in preserving the physical mementos of the past, *An Ounce of Preservation* . . . is a valuable resource . . . If you learn nothing else from this book, you will come away knowing that some of the common things that we do to 'preserve' our old and cherished photographs and letters, such as laminating them, putting them in standard plastic photo albums or even hanging them in a well-lit room, can cause irreversible damage to these items . . ."

— Tamie Dehler,
"Genealogy," *Tribune-Star* (Terre Haute, IN)

"From Junior's most modern collection of X-Men Pogs and Slammers to Great Aunt Margaret's hand-illustrated family genealogy, important personal papers are decaying, fraying and aging into just so much dust. But it doesn't have to be that way, says professional archivist and author Craig Tuttle . . . written in plain language for the average person with a family collection. Interest in family document preservation surged after Ken Burns' documentary on the Civil War which was widely played on PBS stations nationally . . . relied on family collections of photos, letters, and other personal documents to tell the story. After watching the show, many people realized they had similar documents in the attic . . . People also realized those documents were fragile, and they had no idea how to protect them. Tuttle's book has clearly filled a need . . . Someday, those letters penned during the Viet Nam or Gulf wars, - and yes parents, even those X-Men Pogs - may be fodder for the history disks. But, future historians won't be able to scan them onto a multi-media virtual-reality miniature CD if all that's left is dust."

— Laurel Van Leer,
"Books," *The Home News* (NJ)

"Tuttle offers up-to-date suggestions on how to responsibly care for your family possessions. His instruction goes beyond the usual messages and includes ideas on organization, with examples shown . . . his recommendations for preservation are timely."

— "The Tree Tracers," Vol. XIX, #3

"We often talk about gathering up family diaries, pictures, letters, Bibles, certificates and putting them in a central place. But we often do no know how to safely store these items . . . A very useful book . . . "

— Ann Burton,
"Genealogy Gems," *The Decatur Republican* (MI)

"There must be countless attics and basements in this country that contain fragile, priceless documents and pictures - whether that worth is monetary or just sentimental. The tragedy is that too often these unknown heirlooms perish before they are found. More tragic is finding such gems and enjoying them for a time, only to see them ruined because of a lack of proper maintenance and preservation. This book can make such unfortunate events a thing of the past . . . an easy-to-read format . . . The links to our past are one of our most valuable possessions as families, communities, a nation and as humans. They provide insight into our past that is beyond any price tag, and preserving these items should be a paramount concern of anyone who possesses them. Tuttle's offering makes that easy."

— *Southern Book Trade*